PRAISE FOR *Thirst*

"Beautiful and deftly written and intimate and searing in its honesty, Anish's is a quest to conquer the trail and her own inner darkness."

—*Foreword Reviews*, *starred review

"With humility and vulnerability, Heather 'Anish' Anderson reminds us that the most impressive feats of strength and endurance are entirely human endeavors, achieved one step at a time. *Thirst* takes the reader to the trail, but also to the heart."

—Ben Montgomery, author of *Grandma Gatewood's Walk*

"Heather Anderson's book is much like her extraordinary trail accomplishments: extremely personal yet universally inspiring. She exposes the value of following a path apart from the mainstream, and convinces readers of their own ability to unleash personal reserves of endurance to push beyond mental limitations and cultural expectations."

—Jennifer Pharr Davis, author of *The Pursuit of Endurance*

"Just like Heather thru-hikes the PCT from Mexico to Canada, you will thru-read *Thirst* cover to cover for insight into her impressive accomplishments."

—Gina Lucrezi, founder of Trail Sisters

"*Thirst* is the kind of book that sits in your bones. It makes you want to push harder at whatever it is you do. Anish is possibly the greatest athlete in the world, but she didn't start that way. This book gives you hope and courage by showing that no matter who you are or where you are at now, you can do more."

—Liz "Snorkel" Thomas, author of *Long Trails: Mastering the Art of the Thru-Hike*

"In no uncertain terms, Heather 'Anish' Anderson is a legend in the long-distance hiking community. *Thirst* delivers an emotional, inspiring, and beautifully written narrative about the achievement that first put her on this map."

—Zach Davis, editor-in-chief of *The Trek*

Thirst

2600 MILES to HOME

HEATHER "ANISH" ANDERSON

**MOUNTAINEERS
BOOKS**

MOUNTAINEERS BOOKS is dedicated to the exploration, preservation, and enjoyment of outdoor and wilderness areas.

1001 SW Klickitat Way, Suite 201, Seattle, WA 98134
800.553.4453, www.mountaineersbooks.org

Printed in the United States of America
Distributed in the United Kingdom by Cordee, www.cordee.co.uk

22 21 20 19   2 3 4 5 6

Copyeditor: Laura Lancaster
Design and layout: Jen Grable
Cartographer: Martha Bostwick

Cover photograph: *Pacific Crest Trail, Washington* © UT07/iStock

Library of Congress Cataloging-in-Publication Data is on file for this title at https://lccn.loc.gov/2018033393

Mountaineers Books titles may be purchased for corporate, educational, or other promotional sales, and our authors are available for a wide range of events. For information on special discounts or booking an author, contact our customer service at 800-553-4453 or mbooks@mountaineersbooks.org.

♻ Printed on recycled paper

ISBN (paperback): 978-1-68051-236-6
ISBN (ebook): 978-1-68051-237-3

An independent nonprofit publisher since 1960

TO THE TRAIL

for being my comfort when I was broken,
my crucible when I needed to become strong,
and my home without fail.

Map of Important Places on the Pacific Crest Trail

CONTENTS

AUTHOR'S NOTE

All descriptions, events, and dialogue described in this book are based on my personal memories, journals, and discussions with others. Any errors or misinterpretations are mine alone. In a few instances names have been changed to protect privacy.

CHAPTER 1
MISSION CREEK, CALIFORNIA

DAY 8 / 44 MILES

I stood in disbelief for several moments. The creek was bone dry. After I turned on my phone and waited for it to check my location, I could feel my stomach churning and sinking. I already knew that I was in deep trouble.

A few seconds later, Halfmile's app confirmed my fears. The scorching heat of June in Southern California had rendered the crowdsourced water report, updated by Pacific Crest Trail (PCT) thru-hikers, out-of-date in just a few weeks. The muddy ground I'd crossed a mile before was the last "flowing" water in Mission Creek for miles. Nearly out of water, all that stretched before me was exposed canyon and thousands of feet of elevation gain in the middle of the day.

I wanted to cry. Either I would have to backtrack several miles to the last creek bed with reliable water or climb onward into the afternoon sun without anything to drink. Neither option was good.

It was a gamble to walk away from sure water, but it would be a waste of precious time and strength to go backward. Only eight days into my attempt to set the Fastest Known Time (FKT) on the PCT, I already felt like I was fighting a losing battle. "Reliable" water sources were turning out to be dry, and I kept underestimating how much water I needed to carry. No matter how much I thought I'd drink, I always needed more.

Demoralized by the thought of going backward, I put my phone away and stubbornly turned up-canyon. "There must be water up ahead somewhere," I said aloud.

After another hour of hiking in the triple-digit heat without water, my head was swimming. *It was 80 at dawn. This is why no one hikes through Southern California on the PCT in June.* There were supposed to be two more water sources between the dry crossing of Mission Creek and the spring at the head of the canyon, so I kept plodding onward, trying not to think about death by heatstroke or dehydration.

My throat became so dry it was difficult to swallow. I pulled out a stick of gum and chewed until saliva flowed and eased the discomfort. When that piece of gum became hard, I put another in my mouth. For the next hour I chain chewed gum, but eventually even my salivary glands dried up.

Feeling wobbly, I berated myself for not drinking more water the day before. For not carrying more from Ziggy and the Bear's house. For not drinking more from the first Mission Creek crossing. On and on, I identified ways I could have prevented this precarious death march through a desolate canyon in the heat.

A strange plant blocked my path. It had a profusion of pinkish blossoms and an odd, skunky odor. My brain was slow trying to comprehend it, but something in the back of my mind told me to stop. I stood there numbly in front of the alien plant until my brain caught up with my instinct . . .

Poodle dog bush.

I had forgotten all about it in my desperate march toward water. In fact, I didn't even know I might encounter it here. Poodle dog bush has a surface irritant related to poison ivy, yet far more potent. Many people have intense reactions and even need to be hospitalized after contact. Often one of the first plants to revegetate after a forest fire, poodle dog bush had covered several large, recent burns along the PCT. Its potential for aggressive reactions made it something of a boogeyman for aspiring thru-hikers, spawning dozens of online discussions. It scared me so much, I'd marked the locations on my maps. But I didn't recall anyone mentioning it in Mission Creek.

In a daze, I found a stick and pushed the branches aside. I climbed up loose sand and skirted the bush without touching its potentially dangerous leaves. Once past, I saw that the majority of the plants grew only on the slopes above and below the trail. Thankfully . . .

Not long after, I entered a beautiful stretch of canyon lined with cottonwood trees. I'd seen their crowns from a distance and had been striving toward them. Cottonwoods always mean water. *This had to be the next source.*

I left the trail and walked straight up the sandy creek bed. A slick water mark staining the sand made my heart leap with joy. I followed it to a slight overhang along the bank, expecting to find a clear, cold pool.

Instead, I found a small puddle of water with an enormous pile of horse shit in it.

Devastated, I returned to the PCT and shuffled onward. I was so angry. How could the only bit of water for miles be completely contaminated by a horse? I consoled myself by thinking that even if I had wanted to scoop from it, it was too shallow. As I climbed away from the trees and into the sun again, the headache I'd had for hours grew worse until I couldn't think at all. I could no longer fight the urge to sit. My legs folded beneath me without permission and I crumpled into the sand in the middle of the trail. Thin shade from some scraggly bushes seemed like an immense blessing.

I reached for my phone again and turned it on before sinking backward against my pack, reclining on the trail. When my location appeared, I realized I was still several miles from the spring at the head of the canyon.

I lay there in the middle of the trail for what seemed like an eternity. I pondered whether to wait for the coolness of night to continue, but decided that I would likely be in worse shape after seven hours in the heat, with moisture constantly escaping every pore of my body. I needed to get up and keep walking, yet I felt too drained and too defeated by the circumstances.

There was only one obvious answer.

I pulled out my SPOT tracking beacon and opened the cover on the SOS button. All I had to do was push it and help would come. Local emergency personnel would receive my coordinates almost instantly. They would bring me fluids. Fly me to safety. I would sleep in a cool room and eat and drink until my body recovered. I wouldn't have to walk anymore. I could forget that I'd ever attempted this.

"I might die of thirst out here," I said to the orange SPOT in my hand.

CHAPTER 2
SOUTHERN TERMINUS

On June 6, I boarded a plane and flew from Seattle to San Diego, soaring over the length of the mountain ranges I would soon traverse on foot. As the plane swooped over brown hillsides and stucco homes with tile roofs, I realized how very far I was from Washington, which had become my home. Staring east, where clouds and ridges were visible, faint and low on the horizon, I remembered the last time I was here, eight years younger and vastly inexperienced. I had faced the same distance, but this time I knew the enormity of the land extending between myself and Washington. I felt the pull of the mountains I knew like friends, and the people there that I loved.

A small voice inside me whispered, "All that's left to do then is walk."

DAY 1 / 42 MILES

Two days later, I stood at the southern terminus of the Pacific Crest Trail. Three square wooden pillars marked one end of the trail where it met the border with Mexico, just outside Campo, California. Seeing the monument peeling from years of baking in the desert sun, I wondered if I had enough sunscreen. It was barely 6 a.m. and I was already sweating lightly. The friends who'd driven me to the trailhead were excited. I was scared to death. I wasn't sure why I had decided to attempt to set a Fastest Known Time on the PCT. *When most people hit age thirty their crisis involves spending a lot of money—not hiking over forty miles a day alone across the country.* I pretended to make sure I had everything in order to delay the inevitable.

When I had stalled as long as I could, I wrote my intention vaguely in the register, *"Well, here goes."* After a moment's thought I decided that, for posterity, I should make it a little clearer. I added in smaller print to the side, *"To Canada!"* I couldn't bring myself to state that I was attempting a record hike because I was certain that I would fail.

I closed the book and my friends took some pictures. Standing in front of the monument as I stared at the desert, I recalled how foreboding it had seemed last time. But right then, looking at the bare landscape dotted with scraggly bushes and cacti, I remembered that the desert is beautiful too. Finally, I could stall no longer. I strode confidently for my friends even though inside I was screaming *I can't do this!*

I was embarking on a relentless quest that was quite possibly more than I could handle. I'd never consistently hiked forty miles per day before and yet now I intended to do so for two months straight without taking a single day off. Although I'd become an ultramarathon runner over the prior three years, I hadn't done a multi-thousand-mile trek in over six. I'd been in my early twenties then—still full of the unquenchable energy of a child. Now, I was over thirty, and far removed from the life of a mile-crushing nomad. I imagined what it would be like the day I gave up, stuck out my thumb, and rode into town. Tears tracked down my face. *I'm anemic, I haven't been running or training in months, I've never done miles like this . . . What am I doing here?* The slight ache in my left knee reminded me why I hadn't been able to run or train for months. Despite a multitude of doctors and specialists visits, I still had no idea what was wrong with it. I'd run out of patience with my own body. I needed this hike, even if I didn't know precisely why. A knee injury and anemia were not enough to keep me off the trail.

As the Pacific Crest Trail wove past the tiny hamlet of Campo and into the Southern California desert, I was surprised to feel a sense of fluidity in my body. Soon, the trail was gliding underfoot, despite the heat and the weight of my water-laden pack. All the worry melted away. *I am home. Everything is gonna be OK.* My stomach was full of butterflies and yet there was no longer any dread or worry or fuss. I was finally walking. Whatever was to be would be. There was nothing more to think about except putting one foot in front of the other and drinking deeply of the natural world around me. I'd walked this trail once before, as well as thru-hiked the Appalachian Trail and Continental Divide Trail. It had been a long time, but my body had not forgotten the rhythm of the day in, day out of crossing the country on foot. The half decade I'd spent trying to conform to society was a charade. Hiking was my reality. Walking into the desert alone felt like waking up from a long nightmare. With each step, I felt closer, not only to my home in Washington, but also to my true self.

I saw the rattlesnake long before it perceived me. Its three-foot length was sprawled nonchalantly across the dusty track as it basked in the mid-morning sun. After all, the herds of northbound hikers, having mostly started in April, were long gone. The rattlesnake had no reason to expect another hiker. I stopped and backed up, fumbling for my phone to take a picture. Instantly, the snake was coiled and rattling, somehow gliding sideways off the trail in a ready-to-strike position. I laughed as it vanished into the scrub, realizing the irrationality of my fears. Everything about living in the wilderness seems so terrifying from the comfort of a home. Yet, on the trail, nothing is ever as scary as it once seemed.

"Distance makes the heart grow fearful," I said in the general direction of the snake as I passed by.

I reached Hauser Canyon, which was bone dry. Passing by trees clustered near where water once flowed, I remembered when my partner and I had gotten water here in May of 2005. The desert had been much more welcoming then—an abnormally cool and wet spring. We'd never lacked for water or suffered too much beneath the sun. I already knew that this first seven hundred miles—until I entered the High Sierra—were not going to be anything like my last journey. California was in the death grip of a drought and I was crossing parched land just as summer was burgeoning.

The average thru-hiker—one intending to hike the entire Pacific Crest Trail in one season—would work up to walking twenty or so miles per day. An April start would get them to Washington in September, just in time to dodge early fall snows. I would be moving twice that fast. My start was timed so that I didn't hit lingering snow in either the High Sierra or the Pacific Northwest. The sacrifice necessary to have snow-free travel through the high mountains was to sweat my way across the desert long after spring rains had subsided.

After the laborious climb up from the canyon floor, I relished the descent to Lake Morena. I moved quickly, eager to hit the halfway point of my day. When I reached the campground hugging the shore of the wide lake, I refilled my water bladder from a faucet. Very few people were outside. Most were hiding from the heat. The hum of generators running AC units in every RV drowned out the sound of anything else. I felt out of place standing there drenched in sweat. Hot and a little tired, I poured water over my head and braced myself for another twenty miles. But I also felt awash with a sense of accomplishment. I was on pace to reach my camp before nightfall.

As the temperature rose, I found it harder to focus. The terrain began to meld into one long stretch of scrub, brown, and sand. I vaguely marked my progress by road crossings. I kept moving even though I felt dizzy. Thirty miles passed, then thirty-five . . .

I started encountering race markings. I knew the San Diego 100 was taking place in the area and I felt confident that, at any minute, runners would fly past me. My pace slowed as I began to climb. The landscape was stark and the heat unrelenting. No runners materialized. I felt a deep hollowness forming in my gut. *There is no one out here. No one but you. It's too hot. You shouldn't be here either.*

It was the same voice of fear that had spoken up repeatedly throughout my preparations—practicing setting up my new tent, weighing my clothing, purchasing six pairs of trail runners, packing and mailing numerous resupply boxes full of food, batteries for my headlamp, and maps. It was warning me that I was doing something stupid. The night before I'd left, I could not sleep. The voice of fear kept me awake. So, I dealt with it the best way I knew how—I sat down at my computer and wrote in my blog.

I have been called fearless. Brave.

But the truth is, we all have our fears and I am no different.

Words that have always given me perspective and pushed me forward: "Courage means being afraid, but going on anyhow," writes Dan Rather.

I was a scaredy-cat as a little girl. I was afraid of the dark, of ghosts, wild animals, spiders, getting lost, the water, sharks, aliens, rejection, failure . . .

Somewhere along the way I learned to stop letting fear stop me. And that has made all the difference. It has taken me on 3.5 thru-hikes. It has taken me into and out of relationships. Career changes. Race distances in the triple digits. I have been afraid of them all, and yet, each has made me stronger as I overcame those fears.

I am still afraid of many things. Some days it seems like an inconceivable notion that I sleep in the woods alone. That I have faced grizzly bears, wolves, bobcats, rattlesnakes, advanced hypothermia, dehydration, etc. That I routinely risk security in finances and relationships to pursue a life that John Muir would be proud of.

I wonder daily what I am thinking taking on a task so huge. A challenge so big. Who am I to think that I can do this?

Even so, I will step onto the trail and face fear. Fear of:

Rattlesnakes

Heat exhaustion

Dehydration

Pain

Injury

Cougars

Things that go bump in the night

Hunger

Failure.

Scenarios run through my head constantly. Ways I could die out there. Ways I could fail. How hard it will be to press on. How easy quitting will feel. Wondering how the exhaustion of finishing 1,000 miles in 3 weeks will feel when I know I have 1,700 more to go. The numbers scare me. Can I really do this?

The truth is, I don't know if I can or not. However, I think I can,
and that is more than half the battle.

At last the sun began a downward trajectory. The trail wound up into pine forests as I ascended the rolling Laguna Mountains whose rain shadow formed the Anza-Borrego Desert to the east. Wind sighed through the boughs and I breathed deeply. The scent made me ache with longing for the soft pine needle beds I'd spent so many nights on over the years and I felt reinvigorated with desire. With dusk rapidly gathering, I walked faster in the cooling air.

DAY 2 / 49 MILES

When the alarm went off at 5 a.m., I sprang up and packed. Despite not eating dinner the night before, I wasn't hungry for breakfast. I bolted down the trail, eager to put as many miles in as I could before the heat returned. *Yesterday was sweltering—at least 95 degrees.* As I walked the crest of the range, I reveled in the beauty of the Anza-Borrego Desert at sunrise, bathed in perfect morning light. The eastern slopes plummeted to the desert floor, thousands of feet below. From where I walked, it looked smooth and golden—like a field of California poppies in full bloom. As the trail swung westward, I began to encounter oncoming runners.

I cheered for each. Some cheered for me. I was impressed by their run and they were impressed by seeing a thru-hiker. The camaraderie of these ultra-endurance athletes encouraged me. I'd run multiple hundred-mile races myself. I knew the runners' thoughts, emotions, and pain firsthand. It wasn't all that different from what I experienced the previous day as I'd passed the forty-mile mark.

In the late morning, I came to the Pioneer Mail Trailhead parking lot, which was also an aid station for the San Diego 100. Large, white canopy tents filled the space. Runners were trailing in and out while volunteers passed out drinks, food, and first-aid supplies. I spotted trash cans and walked over, eager to toss out the empty wrappers I had. Silly, really, but the few grams of dead weight weighed on my mind more than on my back. I hesitantly asked a woman wearing a volunteer shirt if I could throw away my trash in their bins.

"Of course! Would you like anything to eat?"

"No thanks," I said. I had plenty in my pack. In fact, I'd only eaten a third of what I should have by that point.

"What about a cold Coke?" asked another woman.

I accepted the drink, but refused to take a seat. I felt the seconds ticking away inside my head.

As I guzzled the sweet, icy treat, I listened to the volunteers talk about the record number of runners dropping from the race during the previous afternoon. The temperature had hit 120 degrees. My stomach did a flip-flop. No wonder it had felt *so* hot. They looked at me.

"It's supposed to be the same temperature again today," a man said. "Load up on fluids and electrolytes." With that warning on my mind, I said goodbye and hiked onward.

I encountered a string of runners over the next few miles, and then there was no one. Alone in the desert again, I shuffled along the hot sand. A line of clouds directly above the ridge I was following did little to diffuse the harsh UV, but it was something at least. I imagined my mom at home, washing dishes over the stainless-steel sink and looking out the window at the weeping willow tree swaying in the summer breeze. She'd be praying right now for shade over her baby girl. Tears welled up. I wiped them away and pressed on. It was only my second day on the trail and yet I felt exhausted from the emotional roller coaster I'd been on in the months leading up to that moment. Trying to maintain optimism when faced with something that was certain to be a complete failure was a tight-rope I was tired of balancing on.

I reached a junction and left the PCT to look for a water tank just across the road. Instead, I found the remains of another aid station. The runners were gone, but it was full of partying volunteers.

"Which way is the water tank?" I asked them.

"You need water? Here!"

They offered me as much water and soda and food as I could hold. I drank another Coke and filled my water, but, again, had to decline their offers of food. I just was not hungry, and there was already uneaten food in my pack. A day's worth of food weighed about two pounds. I'd eaten about half a day's worth in a day and a half. Throwing the extra two pounds into the trash seemed like a good idea, but what if my appetite caught up with me?

I poured water into my water bottle and bladder, threw away the wrapper from the single granola bar I'd eaten so far that day, and thanked them. They cheered for me as I left to return to the PCT. I relished the attention and the human interaction. I hadn't anticipated feeling lonely so soon.

Back on the trail, I plodded through the sand and the heat. Again and again, I climbed a ridge and descended. The sun beat down on me and I felt as though I would melt—or, at the very least, my brain would. As I fought to make progress against the wind, I felt a familiar concentrated heat on the side of my heel. A blister was forming.

When I reached the next water tank on the flank of Granite Mountain, I sat in its paltry shade, pulled off my sock, and looked. The skin was already puffed with fluid. Not much I could do now. I put my sock back on. I took stock of my water and decided to bypass the tank, figuring I had plenty to get down to Scissors Crossing and San Felipe Creek.

As I wound along the shadeless mountainside, far in the distance, I could see the brown trail slicing across the bare, gray slope. I descended slowly toward the ancient alluvial plain that fanned from the mountain's gullies across the desert floor. Soon I realized that my "plenty of water" was rapidly diminishing. I still had no idea how much water I needed to walk these distances in the extreme heat, and my westward progress in the heat of the day was sucking me dry.

I came to San Felipe Creek only to find that it was nothing but a sandy wash. Questionable red water had flowed here in 2005, and I'd been counting on it again this year. I realized I wouldn't be able to let my guard down in the desert this year—yet determining just how many liters that guard equaled would still require some trial and error.

I considered my options as I floundered through loose sand toward the highway crossing. I could walk into Julian a few miles away and get water there, or I could press on to the cistern by the Third Gate in the hills ahead. Under the highway overpass I saw hundreds of gallon jugs and I walked toward them as a moth to flame. It was a giant water cache left there for thru-hikers by an anonymous person. Some of the caches along the PCT were in the same location year after year, some were only infrequently managed. As I sat down and flipped through the register full of thank you notes from the hikers ahead of me, I remembered that this cache had been mentioned in the water report. Beat from the miles and the heat, my mind wandered to blankness.

A few minutes later I realized I was staring at the register without comprehension. I looked at my watch. It wasn't even 5 p.m. yet and I'd covered almost forty miles. I poured half a liter of water into my hydration bladder. *I couldn't possibly go through that much in the next thirteen miles to the water tank at Third Gate . . . could I?* It would be dark soon, and cooler. I chugged the water I'd just poured and replaced it with the same amount.

It was soon obvious that I had again misjudged my water needs. Five miles from the cache, my water was gone. I was drenched in sweat and my pack worked in conjunction with gravity to pull me backward at every stride. Everything felt like a fight. I hadn't peed in hours.

I strained my eyes looking for the Third Gate until darkness fell. I had no water, but at least it was finally cool. I pulled my headlamp out of my pack and slipped it on—my first real night hike. Every few minutes, I nervously looked around for mountain lions, fearful of every noise. I became keenly aware of how lonely I was in this big, open landscape. I knew that my fear of them was irrational, that people who had hiked many more miles than me had never seen one. Yet, the elusive cat embodied my fear. They both lurked out of sight, pouncing only when they deemed their prey defenseless.

Has it really only been two days? It felt like it had been a week. Washington seemed like another planet. I imagined what my friends were doing in their daily routines right then—getting home from work, eating dinner, playing with their children. I couldn't quite comprehend that others were proceeding through their days without real physical difficulties, when I was struggling. I finally stopped to pee: it was a deep orange.

I heard the familiar sound of two rattlesnakes to the left of the trail. I couldn't see them, even when I panned my headlamp across the sand. I stood uncertain for about thirty seconds. Finally, I sprinted past the rattling. The noise died off and I returned to a walking pace. Soon, I reached the saddle by the Third Gate and scoped out the camping. I jumped each time I swung the beam of my headlamp into a new space and discovered a rattlesnake. First a rattlesnake coiled in a campsite. Then a rattlesnake on the edge of the trail. They seemed to be everywhere I looked.

Walking quickly, I descended from the PCT while sweeping my headlamp around, looking for the cover of the in-ground water cistern. Near it, I spotted a huge water cache. It only took a few seconds to decide on the fresh water right in front of me over scooping water out of the tank. A sweep of the area revealed it to be snake-free and I set up my tent, dragging a gallon jug inside with me. Then I drank and drank and drank.

CHAPTER 3
VICARIOUS ADVENTURER

Growing up, I was overweight, inactive, and introverted—a bookworm of the highest order, elementary school teachers would find my Nancy Drew books nested inside textbooks—my eyes glued to storylines rather than their instruction. Sometimes they took them away and lectured me about paying attention. Most of the time they let me be. I was reading at a college level by age nine and earning straight A grades. When I wasn't reading, I was weaving my own adventure stories in longhand in piles of notebooks by my bed.

I read and I read. I traveled and journeyed and adventured with Madeleine L'Engle's characters, with Nancy Drew, Huckleberry Finn, Louisa May Alcott's *Little Women*, and, eventually, into the worlds of J. R. R. Tolkien, Diana Gabaldon, and Lewis and Clark. Sacajawea was my own personal heroine. I felt a connection with her through my great-great-grandmother—an Anishinaabe woman whose faded tombstone bore the name "Elizabeth." Through these books, I traveled from an early age through history and around the world without leaving the couch.

MICHIGAN / MAY 1992

"How far did you run, Anderson?" my fifth-grade gym teacher barked, looking up from his notebook, with a pen poised.

I sucked wind and tried to answer without gasping.

"All eight laps."

I was a sweaty, hot mess. Most of the other kids were already heading back toward the brick school building, having finished the two-mile run in far less than the fifty minutes we had for gym. My two best friends were waiting for me by the chain-link fence, and probably had been for at least fifteen minutes.

"No, you didn't."

I stared at him in horror.

"What?"

"You didn't. Don't lie to me."

"I'm not! I ran all eight!"

"Get out of my sight."

Hot tears ran down my flushed face as I hurried to catch my friends. He didn't believe me! It had been the hardest thing I'd ever done . . . and he didn't believe me. I knew it was because I was fat. He knew I hated gym class and, more so, that I hated running. And fat girls can't run two miles. Everyone knew that.

After school, I walked into the house and threw my backpack on the floor. The kitchen smelled deliciously like cornbread. I folded back the towel and cut a four-inch square right out of the middle of the dish of golden goodness. *Still warm.* I smeared it with honey and butter.

My mouth was full when my dad walked in.

"Have you been running laps around the house?"

I nodded, feeling incredibly stupid. Fat girls can't run.

"Maybe try running on the road for a while. You're wearing a path in the grass." He started laughing.

"Don't worry. I won't be running around the house anymore."

What was the point, anyway? I had run daily for a month, training in secret. Today was supposed to be the day I proved my potential athleticism. Or at least that I could do the bare minimum required to pass gym class. And it hadn't mattered at all. Fat girls can't run. Even when they did, no one believed them.

"Yesterday's participation was terrible!" Our sixth-grade gym teacher paced back and forth in front of us. I looked over at my friend and she shrugged.

"I'm embarrassed by you. All of you. I don't know what to do to get you to take exercise seriously."

I lost track of his tirade as I marveled at the ridiculousness of his tie-dyed, zebra-striped balloon pants. He looked like one of the pro wrestlers my dad mocked on TV. *How does he not know how idiotic he looks?*

"So today we're going to write. Yes, write. All athletes need to be able to spell out their goals." He passed out sheets of paper and pencils.

I squirmed around, uncomfortable in my sweatpants. Just sitting still I was hot. My mom had bought them for me after I came home crying because I couldn't handle being teased about my unshaven legs when I wore shorts to gym class. *Why on earth did he have us get dressed for exercise if he was only going to have us write something?* I took my sheet of paper and pencil, passing the rest along. For once, I had a realistic chance at earning an A in gym class.

"Full page from everyone before you leave. Tell me what your current athletic ability is. Your strengths and weaknesses. What you want to achieve athletically and how you're going to get there."

"What if I don't want to achieve anything?" I whispered to Melissa.

"What was that, Anderson?"

"Nothing."

Everyone started scribbling while our gym teacher continued pacing. I wrote my name at the top and chewed on the eraser. I glanced around. Most of the boys were done within five minutes. I could see the papers of many of the girls and they were almost done too. Most of them played some sort of sport, which gave them something to write about.

I'm not in very good athletic shape.

At least starting out the essay was easy: my many athletic weaknesses took up half the page. I wrote big and simply listed every sport I'd ever tried and failed at. When it came time to list my goals and how I would achieve them, I was stumped. I didn't have any. I doodled in the corner of the paper as our gym teacher collected pages from two-thirds of the class.

"Go ahead and change when you're done. You can have the rest of the period free."

The few kids that remained upped the speed of their writing. I closed my eyes and wondered if he'd keep me late. I tried to imagine myself doing anything athletic. Instead, all I could think of were my failures. My father walking away from me, shaking his head and throwing his hands in the air. Leaving me standing there with the ice skates. With a baseball bat. With a golf club, a basketball, a broken kite . . . the list was long. But, I needed to write something. I let my imagination run wild. I was never going to actually achieve anything athletic, but I could write anything.

> *If I ever manage to overcome my athletic weaknesses, I want to set a record. Not just any record, but an athletic record. One that everyone will know me for. One that my dad will be proud of. I don't know what it will be, but I will do it. I have a lot of weaknesses, but I have two critical strengths. I am stubborn and I am smart. I will find a way to be good at something athletic. I will lose weight. I'll get faster and stronger. Maybe I'll even go to the Olympics. Whatever it takes to achieve my goal.*

I was the last student still in the gymnasium when I handed my paper to the gym teacher. I didn't look at him and tried to hurry away.

"Wait."

He was reading the paper right there in front of me. I felt my face growing hot as I stared at my feet. He was going to tear it up and make me rewrite it. I knew it. I couldn't even pass a gym class essay. He knew I was making up something ridiculous just to finish the assignment.

He lowered the paper and handed it back to me.

"Good job."

I ran for the locker room. That night, I taped the essay to the wall beside my bed.

CHAPTER 4
SAN FELIPE HILLS, CALIFORNIA

DAY 3 / 38 MILES

I was already awake when my alarm went off at 5 a.m. The throbbing in my legs had kept me up most of the night, the result of the sudden, intense demands I was placing on my muscles. I'd never experienced pain like this before, and hoped it would eventually go away. My arm searched around for my smartphone, the first one I'd ever owned. It was my camera, alarm clock, and navigation system all in one. If there was ever a multiuse piece of gear, this was it.

Between the heat and the grit, I could barely pry my eyes open. Prolonged dehydration was taking a toll, and I sucked on the hose coming out of my hydration bladder. At last my eyelids parted and I rolled to a seated position. It didn't take long to place my few possessions inside my backpack. Aside from a gray, cuben fiber tent that weighed a mere pound, I carried, among other things, a beat-up sleeping bag that had crossed the country with me on two other thru-hikes, a water bladder, a SteriPEN for sterilizing water, a set of merino wool base layers to sleep in, and my hiking clothes—a white, homemade, long-sleeve blouse and a thrift-store skirt with pink and green candy stripes. A ziplock baggie with antibiotic ointment and medical tape served as my first-aid kit. Mostly what I carried was water and food. Five minutes later, I tentatively exited my tent, thoroughly checking for snakes before stepping out. I was stiff and sore from head to toe and for the first few hundred yards I lurched and jerked like a broken marionette. Eventually, my muscles warmed up and I regained my rhythm. It was then that I became aware of the glory of dawn in the desert around me.

I soaked up the pastel palette and the mellow sunshine. These moments were fleeting—occurring only in the in-between times—early in the morning and just before nightfall. I exulted in the calm, lonesome quiet. Sunlight forced the shadows into hiding as the desert transitioned from the aliveness of night to the desolation of day.

As the morning progressed, I passed a carefully constructed number, spelled out in small stones alongside the trail: "100." The enormity of the last two days crashed in on me. I had covered one hundred miles in triple-digit temperatures in about fifty-two hours. A surge of empowerment swept over me. Those fifty-two hours had been the most grueling of my life, but I had survived. I wasn't broken. In fact, I would soon be in Warner Springs, my first resupply point.

A few hours later, after I had covered many winding miles across open hillsides, a coyote dashed away from a stream of thick, mucus-like, green slime running next to the trail, and disappeared. I looked down at the water it had been drinking and shuddered. Despite the fact that I was completely out of water—and had been for miles—there was no way I was going to even consider drinking that. I was so tired of being thirsty. So far, my estimates as to how much water I would need had been dangerously wrong. I had the capacity to carry a gallon of water and maybe I needed to do just that. I collapsed my reflective shade umbrella as I passed into the natural shade of a tree-lined corridor. It only cooled me a fraction.

I reached a deserted road and strode purposefully along the heat-softened tarmac. It was sweltering. A community center a short distance from the trail was supposed to have water available for PCT hikers. I walked up to the building and rattled the door. It was locked, even though the sign in the window said it was open. Knowing that the Warner Springs resort, another mile down the highway, had closed in 2012, I left the community center parking lot and focused all of my energy on reaching the post office in town—and on ignoring the sand-paper roughness of my dry throat.

Entering the small building, I felt immediate relief as the air conditioning washed over me. I slid my ID across the counter and asked for the box I'd mailed from home.

"Is there anywhere I can get water?" I asked the clerk when she returned, "The community center seems to be closed."

"There's a picnic table behind here and a hose on the side of the building you can use," she said.

I took my resupply box outside and walked around the building. There was a picnic table . . . in the full sun. After opening my box and dumping the contents out, I pawed through the cookies, granola bars, and candy. The M&M's had melted, but I ate some of them anyway. Most of the food I slid into a pile to leave behind. I was tired of carrying things I wasn't eating.

The water from the hose tasted disgusting. I imagined the number of chemicals off-gassing into it while it lay in the sun. A man who'd passed me in the post office appeared from the other side of the building and handed me a bottle of Gatorade.

"I heard you were out of water."

I thanked him profusely and drank it in two giant gulps. Then I went inside the post office and dumped two-thirds of my food into the hiker box—a free box where hikers can leave behind gear and supplies they don't need for other hikers that do—and walked back down the road. I was only eating a few snacks a day and, although I hated wasting supplies, I hated the idea of carrying pounds of food I wouldn't eat even more. My lack of interest in food was abnormal for the energy I was expending, and I had my suspicions that the heat was suppressing my appetite. I knew that, at some point, I would have to get hungry.

Warner Springs was a ghost town. No one was outside. No cars drove by. With the resort closed down, it seemed a shell of itself compared to 2005. Back then, the hot springs resort had been an oasis for hikers. There had been a gas station and store. There had been people. The memories haunted me. I could hardly believe I was in the same place.

Back at the trail crossing, I spied a man outside the fire station. I walked over to him.

"I'm a PCT hiker and the community center is closed. Is there any place here I can fill up my water bottles?"

The firefighters were generous, inviting me to rest in the shade and take as much water from their spigot as I wanted—water that did not taste like a chemical cocktail. I recovered some of my appetite and took a bite of a granola bar. I choked on its dryness and spit it out. I drank more water and took a smaller bite. As I sat out one of the hottest hours of the day in the blessed shade, two separate firemen came out and plied me with bottles of Gatorade. To save my phone battery, I played with my watch's buttons until the alarm was set for 5 a.m. I also turned on the hourly alarm. Maybe with a reminder, I could manage to take in a small amount of calories more regularly. I shouldered my pack, now holding three and a half liters of water, and stepped inside to thank the firefighters. Then I headed out into the heat of the day—to again cross this arid, exposed terrain that shimmered with mirages and memories.

GRAND CANYON, ARIZONA / MAY 2001

I had never seen the desert before I arrived in Arizona. My only experience with it prior to that had been the black-and-white John Wayne movies my dad watched repeatedly. I expected rippled dunes and scrubland where people crawled on their elbows toward a mirage, only to die of thirst beneath circling vultures.

To my astonishment, it was nothing like that. It was beautiful in a way I had not imagined. Soft colors belied the rugged, rocky terrain. The South Rim was thickly forested with pine trees. Kaibab squirrels, with their tufted ears and fluffy, white tails, ran amok in all directions. From the office, I collected paperwork, the key to my shared quarters, and a stack of uniform clothing before stepping outside to take in my first view of the Grand Canyon.

Even in my sleep-deprived state—having dozed fitfully on the floor of the Las Vegas airport the night before—I was unable to turn away from the view. I sat on a short brick wall for forty-five minutes and stared, transfixed.

By age eighteen, I had read enough of adventure to know that I no longer wanted to simply read about it. I wanted to experience it firsthand. I began by traveling with school and volunteer groups: first to Germany and then Alaska, South Dakota, and West Virginia. My first year of college, I found a brochure advertising volunteer ministry work in the national parks while working an additional summer job. I decided that I wanted to see the Grand Canyon, so I filled out an application and mailed it in. A few weeks later, I not only received an acceptance letter from A Christian Ministry in the National Parks, but my employment packet from Xanterra, the park concessionaire managing the Grand Canyon. I'd be spending my summer living at the South Rim and working in the Yavapai Lodge.

The next day, my new coworkers invited me to hike down into the canyon. Although I was suffering from a raging blood infection in my foot from stepping on a broken fence right before leaving home, the side effects of the antibiotics for that infection, and mild altitude sickness from being above two thousand feet for the first time in my life, I said yes. There was no way that I wasn't going.

I swallowed my morning antibiotics, grabbed a small bottle of water, and put a granola bar in my pocket before following the other four people from our housing area to the Bright Angel Trail. We walked down toward Indian Garden, spiraling through the eons frozen in the rock layers. I was too enthralled by my surroundings to feel the ache in my foot. I couldn't believe such a place existed, nor that I was actually here.

One by one, everyone turned back except one of my roommates. She was determined to reach Indian Garden and I was determined to follow her. She was a collegiate basketball player; tall, willowy, confident, and strong. I was sedentary, overweight, and completely in over my head, but, wanting to be what she was, I refused to stop until she did. The temperature rose as we neared the broad, flat Tonto Platform. My infatuation with the scenery could no longer keep me distracted from the pain in my foot, heat-induced drowsiness, and the cramps in my legs, but I refused to turn back.

We reached the lush oasis of Indian Garden as the sun reached its apex. The large thermometer on a post alongside the trail read 120 degrees. We sat on a bench in the shade for a few minutes, drinking water from the faucet nearby, before beginning our climb back out. I'd never walked more than two miles before in my life—the roundtrip from Indian Garden was going to be at least four times that distance.

The world spun. I felt nauseous. Rest areas with fountains were spaced a mile and a half apart, yet I still ran out of water. My foot, throbbing, was swollen against the straps of my sandals. My head pounded. A mule team approached—a string of animals carting other overweight, sedentary folks down into the canyon. A voice in the back of my head chimed in over the sound of hooves clanking down the trail: *People like you don't hike, Heather. They ride. In cars, on mules, in airplanes.* I leaned against the striated walls to let them pass and prayed not to die. When I started moving again, I could see that my roommate had pulled ahead of me. For some reason, all I could think about was my high school gym teacher. How I'd thrown the shot put in class almost as far as our state record holder. I thought of his repeated requests that I join the track team. He'd seen potential there, somewhere. I put my hands on my thighs and pushed down with every step, focused on not losing sight of my roommate.

I lost all sense of time as we hiked upward. My world was a spinning kaleidoscope of sky and swirling, colored rock layers, with my roommate at the center of my vision. Steadily, I inched upward through time. Finally, we crested the rim of the canyon.

GRAND CANYON, ARIZONA / AUGUST 2001

The Canteen at Phantom Ranch was crowded, even though dinner had ended. Post-meals, non-guests were allowed to relax in the cozy space filled with community games and quite a bit of talk and laughter. I had left my dark campsite near the Colorado River and shyly picked a spot at an empty table to sit and journal. In the midst of writing about my experience descending the Bright Angel Trail that morning, and my afternoon spent building a sand castle on the bank of the Colorado River, a shadow fell across the notebook.

"Mind if I join you?"

I looked up to see a young man with disheveled blond hair and a battered knapsack standing across the table. His accent was decidedly British and his appearance fit my romanticized idea of a world traveler. I was immediately intrigued.

"Of course," I closed my notebook. "I'm Heather."

"Mark."

He plopped down across from me and smiled. "Journaling?"

"Yes, I try and write every day. Have since I was about nine. Although sometimes I don't have much to talk about."

He nodded and fiddled with the cup of water in his hands.

"I keep a journal too. Especially when traveling." He pulled a battered leather journal out of his pack and set it on the table. "It's been to seventeen countries and three continents . . . so far."

"Wow. That's really cool. How long have you been traveling?"

"This is month seven of a planned yearlong holiday. How about you?"

"I'm actually working at one of the hotels on the South Rim for the summer. I wanted to try and hike across the canyon before I leave. So, I hiked down today. Heading to the other side tomorrow."

"Impressive. That's a long day. You must do a lot of tramping."

"Sort of. Day trips mostly. Actually, this is my first overnight. I had to borrow everything from my coworkers."

He sat back into his seat and studied me. For an instant, I thought that perhaps I was making a huge mistake and he was about to tell me to go back up to the South Rim first thing in the morning. Instead, he said, "Hmmm."

His very blue eyes were probably noticing the frayed Velcro sandals, purchased from Walmart, that I'd kicked off next to the clunky external-frame pack I'd borrowed. They weren't exactly hidden from view. He was definitely not dressed in cut-off denim shorts and a cotton T-shirt like I was. Instead, his synthetic khaki pants and loose, long-sleeved, button-up shirt looked like they'd be cool and comfortable in the blazing sun. Not to mention protective. I realized I'd forgotten sunscreen.

"Good luck. It's a pretty big climb, but probably very beautiful. I went partway over there today. To a place called Ribbon Falls."

"That sounds nice. Is it close to the North Kaibab Trail?"

"Oh yes, a short side trip. It's well worth it. I even got to climb right up on the pulpit rock under the falls and take a little shower. Felt like I was on top of the world." He grinned at me.

"I'll have to check that out tomorrow. I can probably afford to do a short side trip. My friends aren't picking me up until 4 p.m."

"You absolutely should. Not planning to hike back across then?"

"No way! Rim to rim to rim is just plain crazy. That's like forty-five miles or something."

He seemed amused by my response and polished off his cup of water. It reminded me of something I'd been worried about all day.

"Is that the only place to get water along the route? The falls? I borrowed this filter and a hydration bladder from a friend, but I'm not sure how much I'll need to carry."

"Oh, you probably won't even need the filter. There are water faucets in the campgrounds and another one at the base of the ascent . . . at the pipe master's house."

"Pipe master?"

"The bloke who lives down here and caretakes the water pipe that runs across the canyon. There's a drinking fountain right in his yard you can fill up at."

"Oh! I have heard of him. I didn't know there was water there."

"There is. If you decide you want to do more tramping in the future, you might get some of these though. It's what I use."

He slid a small, white bottle across the table to me. It had a chemical formula and some warnings written on it, but they were nearly illegible. It was obvious from the wear on the label that he had been carrying them in a pack pocket for at least the seven months he'd been traveling—if not longer.

"What are these?" I held it to my ear and shook it, hearing a rattle.

"Chlorine tabs. You just put one in your water and let it sit for twenty minutes. It sterilizes the water. And, it only weighs a fraction of that filter you're carrying."

"Amazing! Where do you get them?" I pushed the bottle back toward him.

"Keep them. I'm hiking out tomorrow, then heading to Las Vegas. I won't need them there."

"Are you sure?"

He smiled and stood up. "You've got a very long day ahead of you, and many more adventures after that. I won't keep you."

"Oh, thanks. I suppose I should get to bed. I'm going to need to get up early."

"It's dark—would you like me to walk you to your campsite? I have a torch."

I thought of the warning signs about mountain lions, rattlesnakes, and scorpions I'd seen, and the stories I'd heard about them wandering through Bright Angel Campground while campers slept.

"Yes, that would be great."

We walked down the path with elbows linked. He wisely carried a very small light that illuminated the ground almost as much as daylight. I'd never even thought of borrowing a flashlight. Obviously, I still had a lot to learn about hiking. I thanked him again as he left me standing at the edge of my site. He squeezed my arm and wished me a safe journey. I watched his light disappear back toward Phantom Ranch and I shook my bottle of chlorine tablets, smiling as though it was a bottle of gold. My eyes adjusted to the darkness well enough to see the outline of the three-person tent that had taken me over an hour to set up. It seemed much smaller now that darkness enveloped it. The hair on the back of my neck prickled, and I hurried over to the tent and crawled in. I slipped the chlorine tablets into my backpack and closed my eyes.

It was barely light the next morning when I finished shoving the voluminous tent into my pack and hoisted it, first onto my knee, then my back. Kate would be at the North Rim, fourteen miles from where I stood, in ten hours. Much of the trail was straight up, which left no time for dawdling. I passed through Phantom Ranch before anyone was awake, relishing the chill that hung in the air. I knew it wouldn't last.

The last question Mark had asked me before we'd parted ways was if I'd ever hiked fourteen miles before. That was when I first truly realized that my series of five-mile (or less) day hikes over the previous weeks may not have adequately prepared me for what I was in the middle of attempting. Yesterday had been the first time I'd ever carried an overnight pack, and I was bruised from it. I wiggled my shoulders, trying to settle the pack more comfortably on my body. It didn't seem that comfort would be possible.

I tripped. The weight on my back plowed me into the ground with unexpected force—as though I'd been run over by a charging bull. I threw my hands out and they, along with my knees, skidded across the rocks until I stopped. I lay with my cheek in the dust for a few moments, too shocked by the fall to move. I winced as I pushed myself back up, turning to search for the rock that had tripped me. The trail I'd just crossed was surprisingly smooth.

"What the hell?" I looked down at my knees, assessing the damage. Along with the blood oozing from several scrapes, I noticed that the sandal on my right foot was deformed.

I leaned against the rock wall and picked up my foot. The entire sole of the sandal hung loose, attached only at the heel. In disbelief, I lifted my other foot and saw that the sole of that sandal was also peeling back from the toe.

"This can't be happening. I have twelve miles to hike."

I tried to walk a few more steps and nearly tripped over the flopping sole again. In frustration, I tried to tape the soles on with duct tape. Within a mile, the tape had worn through and they were both back to flopping. I set my pack on the ground, sat down next to it, and pawed through it, finding nothing of real use for repairs other than the duct tape and an ankle brace.

I ripped what was left of the sandals off of my feet. Angrily, I stuffed them into my backpack. I yanked the ankle brace onto one foot and wound duct tape around it. I was glad to be carrying half a roll now, despite its weight. Then I entombed the bare foot in tape as well.

I got back up and started walking. I could feel every rock poking into my feet, but the duct tape was some protection. I hoped it would last, since I'd used it all. Soon I reached the turnoff marked "Ribbon Falls." I staunchly refused to let the destruction of my footwear ruin my day. I marched left.

Just as Mark had described, a huge pulpit rock stood under a thin shower of water plummeting down from a brink some distance above. I shrugged my pack off and climbed up behind the falls. The sun had yet to fill the inner gorge and the thought of getting in the cold water did not sound as appealing as it had the night before. I closed my eyes and rushed a few steps forward into the spray.

"Ahhhhhhhhhhhhh!" My scream echoed in the silence as the water pummeled my head and shoulders.

I stepped out shivering. I wasn't sure I'd ever felt so alive before.

By the time I reached the drinking fountain at the pump house a few hours later, the duct tape had completely worn through to the ankle brace and had mostly come unstuck from my bare foot due to sweat. I plopped down next to the fountain and ripped what was left of it off. I rubbed my hands across my sweaty face and neck, pushing back the unbraided hair that clung to them. I was ungodly thirsty. I filled my bottle, drank, and refilled. I poured the second bottle over my head, and then I drank some more. I hadn't even begun climbing yet. Just as I was about to urge myself to stand up and keep moving, a man came out of the nearby ranger house.

"What happened to your boots?"

"Uh, well they were sandals. They fell apart near Phantom Ranch."

"Where are you heading?"

"I'm hiking across the canyon. Rim to rim."

He stared at me, without speaking, for what seemed like an eternity.

"What size shoe do you wear?" he finally said.

"Nine."

"I have a spare pair of boots. You can have them. Let me get them for you," he turned and began to run toward his house.

"No! No, that's OK. It's only six more miles. I'm doing OK."

"Seriously. They are an old pair. I don't mind."

"It's OK, really." My pride had me on my feet with my pack on my back before he could convince me to accept help.

I headed out and up. Mankind had done without shoes for millennia. Surely, I could hike a few more miles. I knew accepting the old boots would have been the smarter option. But I was going to achieve this big, unwieldly goal without help—except for a small bottle of chlorine tablets.

Two hours later, I sat panting on the white sand in the middle of the trail. My head hurt from the heat and my feet were leaving bloody marks on the sand. My scabbed-over knees ached from the fall and the backpack had worn raw sores into my shoulders and back. From where I sat, I could see two sun-bleached sleeping bags fifty feet below me. I wanted nothing more than to toss my entire backpack off the side of the canyon, and someone else had clearly had the same idea on this unrelenting ascent.

I tipped my head back to drink the last of the water I'd carried from the pump house. My watch read 2 p.m. and I was two miles from the top. I put the empty bladder back into the pack and got to my feet. Then I stood for a moment with my hands on my thighs until I stopped seeing stars. Finally, I started hiking.

I felt a burst of energy as the top of the climb came into view. When I reached the trailhead fountain, I dropped down beside it and let water flow straight into my mouth and over my face. Then I let it wash the blood and dirt from my feet. With a smile on my face, I hobbled toward the parking lot. I threw the tattered brace into a trash can at 2:45 p.m. Not only had I crossed the Grand Canyon, I had done so barefoot. And, faster than I thought I could. The same rush I'd felt standing a few hours before in the cold water of Ribbon Falls washed over me.

GRAND CANYON, ARIZONA / AUGUST 2001

My dance with Death began as a shuffle across the Tonto Platform into the midsummer sun. My skin no longer produced sweat and I was certain I was going to die. Temperatures here often soar over 110 degrees and I was completely and utterly without water. Over the previous three months, I had gone from neophyte hiker to canyon explorer, but it had been a steep learning curve.

A large boulder cast a small blob of shade and I collapsed into it, my back sliding down the rock until my butt was in the dirt. My legs flopped outward. I was panting. *How far was it to Hermit Creek? It seems like I should have been there already . . .*

My mind drifted as I stared at the soaring walls of the Grand Canyon. I was not in the main corridor. I was well away from where most people hike and rangers frequently patrol. It was my second overnight trip, and the first one on my own away from the busy Inner Gorge. The weight of my backpack helped cement me to the ground.

"Well God, I guess this is it," I murmured.

The full moon had already risen just above the red stone walls, its whiteness stark against the cerulean sky. I stared, hardly comprehending what I was looking at. *How long had it been since I'd had a drink? Two hours? Three? Maybe more . . . How long have I been sitting here?*

"Thank you for giving me something beautiful to look at, at least, before I go." I closed my eyes, feeling disconnected from my body. I thought about how dehydration kills. It was almost as if I could feel my blood's viscosity increasing in my veins.

I imagined Death extending his hand to me . . . *Do you want to dance?*

I opened my eyes again and pulled strength from the beauty of the moon and sky, from the canyon itself. Something deep inside me pushed back against Death's invitation. I wanted to live.

If I can just make it to the Hermit Creek Junction. It's only one more mile from there. I can make it one more mile. I have to. I must. I can. I cannot die here. I refuse.

Too dehydrated to even say my mantra aloud, I rolled to my side and pushed myself onto my hands and knees. Slowly, dizzily, I pulled myself to my feet using small knobs in the rock. I leaned against the boulder as I shuffled my feet around it, back onto the westward facing trail. The sun's intensity felt like a physical blow. I stumbled to a weather-beaten sign on the other side of the boulder. Grabbing hold, I fought to focus my eyes on it long enough to read: Hermit Creek 1 Mile.

I would have cried if I'd had any fluids left to spare. Stumbling and uncoordinated, I made my way straight into the sun—a floundering mess. After an eternity of telling myself to just keep going, I followed the trail down into a side canyon. Below me crystal clear water poured across rocks as it bounced toward the Colorado River. I threw myself into the creek and lay there, face up, letting the water cascade over my body and into my mouth. Death and I may have had our first dance that day—a drunken waltz through the desert heat—but my dance card was not yet full. I would live to dance again.

INDIANA / SEPTEMBER 2001

I stood in the doorway of my advisor's office. Being back at school in the temperate, green Midwest was a shock after months in the Arizona desert. Dr. Shively was seated at his desk, flipping through what I presumed was the paperwork from my internship. I slipped into his office through the open door.

"Hi."

"Oh, Heather, hello. Right on time. Please sit down."

I sank into the leather chair and pulled my folder out of my backpack. I flipped it open and poised a pen over a blank page to take notes. Three internship credits and my ability to graduate in three years, rather than four, hung on his approval of my summer experience.

"I've read through everything you submitted. Very interesting choice for a ministry internship. Most students choose churches. Working as a volunteer with A Christian Ministry in the National Parks and holding down a full-time job takes a lot of dedication. How did it go for you overall?"

"It was . . . eye opening. Difficult. I worked forty hours a week and participated in all of the worship as well as the group events. And I took up hiking with my spare time."

"Not much of that, I suppose." Dr. Shively smiled.

"No, not really. I didn't sleep much actually."

That was an understatement. I cringed inwardly, thinking of the last worship ceremony of the summer, which I'd led. The night before I'd agreed to hike with a friend from rim to river and back, after we got off work at 6 p.m. I'd known it was a bad idea since she was not a hiker, but she was desperate to do it before her summer job ended—and I was always up for an adventure. We'd crawled into our beds at 5 a.m. Three hours later, unshowered and with my shirt on backward, I was standing in front of the crowd gathered for worship on the canyon rim.

"I see. Well, I know your focus has been missions. How did this internship shape your perception of mission work and your interest in that branch of ministry?"

There it was. The million-dollar question I had skirted in my essay. I had hoped I wouldn't get asked so bluntly. Dr. Shively was an ordained minister, my advisor, and a brilliant professor of religion. I was his A student, Greek scholar and tutor, and questioner of conservative inter-pretations of social and environmental issues in the New Testament. Now I was about to dash his ecumenical hopes for me.

"Well, you see, I, uh, experienced God . . . differently than before. In the canyon itself."

His brow wrinkled ever so slightly. I looked him in the eye.

"You see, I've decided that I don't want to go into the ministry after all. I want to be a vagabond."

To his credit, Dr. Shively looked confused, but he didn't immediately react—at least not outwardly. Finally, after pausing for several moments, he set the papers on his desk and folded his hands.

"A vagabond. So, tell me more about what you mean by that—and how you came to decide that during your internship."

"Well, I went hiking. And we did these services on the rim of the Grand Canyon. And my friends and I drove to Utah to see Zion and Bryce Canyon. All these incredible places touched my spirit in a way I've never felt before. I did some really difficult hikes. I ran out of water when it was really hot. My shoes fell apart and I hiked across the canyon barefoot. I prayed all of those times and for the first time I really felt like someone was listening. I stopped feeling God inside the church. Or with other people. Or really anywhere except when I was out hiking or moving through a landscape. It was like seeing God with my very own eyes instead of closing them and imagining him. I felt like Eve must have when she first opened her eyes and saw the beauty of the garden."

I gushed, in what I hoped was an articulate manner, all the thoughts that had bounced around in my head ever since my first hike into the Grand Canyon. "I realized that I don't feel comfortable telling people to believe what I believe the way I believe it. I don't want to tell people to worship as I do. I realized that what I enjoy about mission work is that I am tangibly helping people. And I still want to do that. But for me, I don't know if I can go back to sitting in a pew. After graduation I've decided to hike the Appalachian Trail. I can't imagine anything better than being immersed in nature for months on end. I don't know how or where I'll end up from there, but it doesn't matter. I'd be happy living in my car and hiking for the rest of my life. The way I feel out there is whole and complete. For once, I found a place where I actually belong and everything feels right. It's all I've ever wanted from life."

His eyebrows arched higher and higher as I talked, until I was certain they'd fold in half. When I finally paused to catch my breath, he lowered them and nodded.

"The natural world is a very powerful representation of God. Just don't confuse the two."

I nodded. I hadn't spoken my thoughts to anyone else and I felt a heady lightness inside my chest as though I'd released something very heavy into space. He picked up my file and closed the folder.

"I think this internship was very powerful for you. Whatever calling you accept I am certain that God is guiding it. I'll be sure to get the forms sent in so that you can receive full credit."

"Thank you, Dr. Shively."

"You're most welcome. I hope this doesn't mean you won't be tutoring my Greek students this year?"

"Oh, of course I will."

He smiled. "I'm glad to hear it."

I walked out of his office almost giddy. Dr. Shively hadn't rejected the honest outpouring of my inner thoughts. I felt a measure of acceptance that I had never felt before. For the first time, someone seemed to accept my alternative way of feeling, believing, and acting. It was OK to be me.

CHAPTER 5
CLEVELAND NATIONAL FOREST, CALIFORNIA

DAY 5 / 43 MILES

Even after days of walking through the desert, bleached by the sun and nearly crazed with constant thirst, I was struck by its variety—in vegetation, animal life, and terrain features. The Pacific Crest Trail weaves three separate desert ecosystems together—the Anza-Borrego, the Sonoran, and the Mojave—each with their own unique personality. Even when the trail is not technically in one of these desert ecosystems, the chaparral, scrub oak, and pines remind you of the dryness of this land.

My experiences in the deserts of the Grand Canyon had changed me forever. The realities were harsh, yet I was in love. I'd begun hiking in a desert and here I was in the desert again, twelve years later, on the cusp of starting my life anew. My ability to survive the arid austerity of the desert had grown since that first day on the Bright Angel Trail. I stayed as hydrated as possible, wore my long sleeves and skirt, and never forgot my sunscreen. Smiling with cracked lips, I surveyed the landscape around me. The desert would always be my first love.

An hour after receiving my diploma in May of 2003, I handed it to my parents, hugged them goodbye, and jumped into a Geo Metro with my two best friends. We drove all night—sleeping for just a few hours—to a remote mountaintop at the end of a rough dirt road in northern Georgia. The three of us walked a mile to the summit and promised to see each other in six months. Then, I started out, intent on walking from Georgia to Maine: 2,200 miles along the Appalachian Trail.

I had no practical experience with multi-night backpacking. It was a steep learning curve, but in my soul, I felt I was doing exactly what I had always been destined to do. I also felt a deep connection with my great-great-grandmother growing within me. I felt her blood pulsing in my veins as I climbed mountain after mountain and hiked mile after mile through thick forest. In the tradition of thru-hikers, I took a trail nickname: Anish—short for Anishinaabe—in her honor.

I went on to hike other long-distance trails over the next three years: the 2,600-mile-long Pacific Crest Trail and the roughly 3,000-mile-long Continental Divide Trail. Then I retired from walking. I married and started a career. To stay sane, I took up long-distance running. Soon I was running thirty, fifty, even one hundred miles through the mountains alone. It filled the void for a while, but, in the end, there was nothing that could replace living in the wilderness for months on end.

My marriage ended in 2011. In the two years that followed, I severed nearly every other tie to society that I'd ever had. After our separation I sold what belongings remained. A year later I quit my job at the software company and left my apartment. I moved into a cabin with no indoor plumbing and only an ancient cast-iron woodstove for heat. Then, I walked back into the mountains, uncertain and questioning. I returned to the PCT, getting on the trail in southern Oregon with the intention of walking nine hundred miles back home. At first the trail was very difficult as I struggled to find my thru-hiking muscles again, but once I did I discovered that the answer to my question was the same as it had been nearly a decade before: this is home.

As that hike drew to a close, I felt a deep urge inside me to embark on an even longer journey through the wilderness. I needed to return to the path I had once walked, but simply walking the trail again was not what I was seeking. I needed a new type of intensity. I needed to pit myself against something I had never faced.

The answer came to me clearly one evening while I lay in my tent: *Hike the Pacific Crest Trail faster than anyone, male or female, has ever done before.* It was both insane and completely logical. Although it was outside the scope of anything I had ever done before, I felt comfortable and at ease with the decision. Just as I had known that I was fulfilling my destiny the first time I thru-hiked, I knew beyond a shadow of a doubt that I was meant to attempt this record, even if I didn't know why. I returned home from the hike and started to research. I found a website that contained information on every Fastest Known Time reported and studied the information diligently. There were standards and loose rules to follow, spelled out on the introductory pages, as well as hundreds of records held on as many trails and routes. Most of the people I didn't know. However, the PCT page assured me that the current record—64 days, 11 hours, and 19 minutes—was held by hiking legend Scott Williamson. I nearly gave up my nascent idea when I read his name. He'd completed many hikes of the PCT including the first yo-yo—hiking from Mexico to Canada and then turning around and hiking back in one continuous trip. Armed with new information, I brooded on the thought of setting an FKT for several months, telling no one about my plan.

Now, with ten miles to go to reach my planned campsite, and overwhelmed with fatigue, I simply wanted to stop. The trail had turned from scrubby hills to a tumultuous landscape of boulders as it wound its way past pale rocks, following ridges that were seemingly endless. Each one folded in upon itself, disguising its true length like a coiled diamondback. I followed the serpentine course, breathing deeply of the vistas all the while lamenting the aches of my body.

"Are you excited for your hike?"

The question that everyone had asked in the weeks leading up to my hike still bounced around inside my head like an echo that wouldn't die. As my departure had grown imminent, I knew that I had to explain my upcoming disappearance from everyday life. In the final months of preparation, I'd begun telling my friends and family about my goal . . . and eventually strangers on long runs. Inevitably, they were superficially interested—few comprehended the actuality of what I planned to do—so I always answered yes, because I knew that I was supposed to, even though I felt more like I was being forced to walk the plank. On trail I didn't feel excitement either, only impetus. The few people I had met gave me effusive praise for attempting this seemingly crazy endeavor. I received it with a mix of emotions, drawing courage and strength as well as resentment from their words. *People believe I can do this! Maybe they are right! Yet, I feel like a sacrifice to vicariousness. If people were this eager to see someone break this record, then why didn't someone else do it already? Why me?*

I didn't know if I had what it took. In fact, I seriously doubted it. But I was unwilling to give up without a fight. After all, I'd quit my job, sold most of my belongings, and bought a one-way plane ticket—my last ditch effort to regain happiness and a purpose in life. *If it doesn't work . . . ?* I supposed I'd throw my past—my identity and my memories—off a cliff and walk away with nothing. Walk away to become someone else—somewhere else—and never look back, never hike again.

As the moon rose and the sky turned lavender my longing to arrive at my campsite grew almost unbearable. There seemed to be no end to these ridges, and as night fell even the magic of the desert sky couldn't keep me moving quickly. I stopped every few hundred yards to lean on my knees. After a few seconds I would walk again, aware that I was moving at a glacial pace as my sleeping hours dwindled away.

I arrived at the saddle I'd been aiming for, relieved to discover that it was broad and flat—an excellent campsite. Exhausted, I set up my tent, crawled in, and collapsed. I was too tired to eat. My legs twitched and buckled as cramps and spasms gripped every muscle. My shoulders and back burned. I tried to sleep, but as with every other night the soreness woke me after only an hour or two.

Too soon, molten gold light poured over the horizon in time with the beeping of my watch. I pried open my eyes and fumbled for my water. I sucked down some of the precious liquid, swallowing with difficulty as it passed my sore throat. I reached for my phone and typed an entry for my blog:

My day starts at 5 a.m. I will walk all day at 3 miles per hour, stopping only to get water, dump sand from my shoes or such. Each stop lasts but a few minutes. I walk until the miles pile up, until night falls and my headlamp comes out, until the aching in my feet and legs seems unbearable. The last miles I am stumbling, tripping. Finally, I pitch my tent on whatever surface is available. It may be flat, or not, or rock hard, but it is home for the next few hours. Inside I choke down a protein shake. Daily, exhaustion overrides my hunger. I peel socks off from blistered swollen feet. I crawl into my sleeping bag and prop my feet on my food bag. Stinging shoots along my nerves: throbbing in my legs and feet makes it hard for me to sleep. I clench my teeth against the jolts and wait for exhaustion to overcome me again. A few hours later, I am awakened by my alarm. Bleary eyed, I wish to go back to sleep, but then I remember all who believe in me, everyone cheering me on. I think of the sticker on the back of my phone which reads 'Never, never, never give up' and the bracelet on my wrist which says 'Nothing great is easy' and I sit up. Bolstered by these reminders, I have the courage to put my battered feet back in my worn-out shoes once again.

CHAPTER 6
SAN JACINTO MOUNTAINS, CALIFORNIA

DAY 7 / 46 MILES

Humans have always gone on journeys. Whether as mass migrations following game or fleeing climatic changes or setting out on vision quests or to establish a new life, as a species, we move. Thousands of people now satisfy this innate human impulse through the long-distance trails of the United States—of which the Pacific Crest Trail, the Appalachian Trail, and the Continental Divide Trail are just a few. These thru-hikers often begin the trail solo, but most find that what they thought would be a lonesome human vs. wilderness experience becomes a chain of shared human connectedness.

I was no different. Even though I walked alone, there were continual reminders that I was not forging a new path. Thousands of people had walked here before, as had I. I passed places where I'd met other hikers that remain my friends to this day. The landscape was full of memories, yet the faces and voices were but apparitions now, mingling with the shimmering waves of heat rising from the ground.

There were other reminders that other people were in this desert with me now, too. Footprints in the sand and water caches in the damnedest places were bits of humanity that lessened my loneliness. There were also the trail angels.

Trail angels start off as people who reside along long-distance trails and become aware of the passage of humanity just beyond their doorsteps year after year. Rather than being put off by the smell, dirt, and transient nature of thru-hikers, trail angels embrace them with open arms, both literally and figuratively.

All along the Pacific Crest Trail there are trail angels who open their homes to hiking vagabonds. They hold packages mailed there for thru-hikers and offer up showers, washing machines, and even their kitchens to complete strangers. These are the tangible blessings that trail angels offer hikers, but the intangible human connection that comes from giving and receiving is a blessing that nourishes the soul.

In the course of accumulating seventeen thousand miles of hiking and running in the mountains, I'd been blessed by these angels in many ways, from food and drink to showers to places to sleep and wash my clothes. Meals had been purchased for me, rides provided, and, perhaps most importantly, beautiful benedictions of encouragement had been spoken over me.

I looked forward to crossing I-10 and reaching the home of Ziggy and the Bear, elderly trail angels who lived a mere stone's throw from the Pacific Crest Trail. All that stood between me and their home was the San Jacinto massif.

The Southern California desert is not flat. It is also not an endless sea of rolling dunes. Rather it's a complex terrain composed of ridgelines, washes, and chaparral scrubland punctuated by massive mountains, and their attendant plateaus, that soar to heights of nearly 12,000 feet above sea level. San Jacinto Peak, at 10,834 feet, is one of those mountains.

For once, the morning did not swiftly give way to hellish temperatures. Despite the effort of my upward trajectory, I felt cool and comfortable. I had again left the scrubland behind and entered whispering pine forests. A surge of optimism overwhelmed me. At first, I couldn't quite identify the new emotion, but at last I realized what it was: I felt *capable*. Perhaps not capable of completing my goal, but at least capable of meeting challenges and solving problems as they came my way.

Despite everything, I was still moving forward. It seemed impossible at times, and yet, here I was.

Finally reaching the crest at nearly nine thousand feet, I enjoyed a long traversing amble despite being out of water. It was a treat to be in a canopy of trees and not dragging myself up or down steep terrain in the blazing sun. When I finally reached the stream I'd been counting on, I was elated to find that it was gushing merrily across the trail. I climbed in—not caring that my shoes were getting wet—and knelt down.

"Oh my God. This is heaven."

I dunked my head into the cold flow. Then I filled my bottle and chugged a liter. Cooled from outside as well as from within, I felt rejuvenated. I cherished the moment, remembering the tortuously long, exposed, and waterless descent to I-10 that lay ahead of me.

It only took a couple of miles for the water to completely evaporate from my shoes and clothing. I crossed the Black Mountain Road and began to descend in earnest. Down, down, down, switchbacking through chaparral that scraped my legs and tore at my skirt. I kept a keen eye on the ground for rattlesnakes. There'd been many the last time I passed through here. I thought of that day as I walked.

"What if I don't recognize the sound of a rattlesnake and I step on it?"

"Trust me, Heather. You'll recognize it."

It was only ten minutes later that I found myself leaping several feet down the trail without even thinking about it. I turned around to stare at my fiancé wide-eyed.

He pointed down to the base of a rock alongside the trail between us. I could just make out the camouflaged coil of a western diamondback.

After carefully descending below the trail tread to avoid further disturbing the snake, Remy clambered up to stand next to me.

"See? I told you that you'd recognize it."

Endless hours and sixteen miles later, I reached the drinking fountain at the Snow Creek Trailhead. The shining metal seemed so foreign as it glinted in the evening light. I held my breath as I turned it on . . .

Water poured out. The gods of dry places had once again seen fit to supply my needs.

The trail followed roads for a while and I alternated between a fast hike and a jog. In the distance, cars raced along the interstate. I knew that just beyond the interstate my next resupply sat waiting in the home of Ziggy and the Bear. It was nearly 9 p.m. and I dug deep to push my pace through the sand so as to not arrive too late and disrespect their generosity.

As darkness fell I hiked beneath the interstate, the thundering above me echoing through the deserted underpass. The slog continued as I skirted a subdivision full of porch lights, barking dogs, and the blue glow of TV screens. Suddenly I felt like a skittish coyote relegated to a life of slipping through shadows on the edge of civilization—removed from its circle.

On the edge of the subdivision I turned off of the trail and tentatively entered the gated yard at 10 p.m. I was thankful that I wouldn't have to sneak around the edges of town again and relieved to see another hiker outside fussing with his gear while the angels sat in their living room watching TV. I tapped lightly on the glass. A small-statured woman with white hair looked up.

"You made it," Ziggy said with a smile. "I'll have the Bear show you where the shower is. I already set your box on the table."

"Thank you," I said to her, as the Bear shuffled over to me. He was bent with age, but I could see from his large frame how he'd gotten his nickname.

"How far did you come today?" he asked as he led me to a small bathhouse a short distance away.

"The other side of the mountain."

"Towels and soap are in there. I'm sorry, but we don't have laundry available here. Not enough water."

"That's fine. Thank you so much."

I washed quickly and thankfully, eager to erase the last two hundred miles of sweat and dust. Water rolled over me as well as gratitude. Once again, I remembered one of the greatest lessons of a thru-hike: the restoration of faith in the goodness of humanity.

Over and over in my journeys, I had been treated with incredible generosity by trail angels such as Ziggy and the Bear, the Saufleys, the Andersons, the Dinsmores, and others who aid all hikers passing through. I'd also been helped by complete strangers who didn't even know about the trail I walked, but wanted to help someone in need, who saw beyond the dirt and stench and connected with the concept of my journey. Countless times my meals had been covered by other patrons of a restaurant; a hitchhike led to a shower, laundry, a meal, and a ride back to the trail, even though it was out of the way; or a place to stay the night developed from a conversation at a grocery store.

I breathed deeply and let out a shuddering breath. What I was doing was solitary, more so than my previous thru-hikes. But, despite my solitude in the effort, I felt more connected to others on and off the trail than I had in a very long time, tapped into the greater ties that bind us all in an ever-widening circle of love. Life felt real again.

CHAPTER 7
MISSION CREEK, CALIFORNIA

DAY 8 / 44 MILES

At 5 a.m. the large thermometer hanging in the shade of the awning read 80 degrees. I got up from where I'd laid down on the ground just outside Ziggy and the Bear's door the night before and threw my gear into my pack. The other hiker was still sound asleep a few feet away. I forced some food into my uninterested body—surprised that it still functioned on less than two thousand calories a day when I was expending five times that much energy. On my way out, I slid the thank you card and donation I'd been carrying into the box by the door. I smiled and silently asked for blessing on the two angels of the desert who were still asleep inside the house. I crept out of the gate and began my ascent into the barren hillsides.

A few hours later I was walking along Whitewater Creek. I reached the ford, which was merely a shallow rock hop, and checked my water supply. Just enough to get me up and over the dividing ridges between the Whitewater drainage and that of Mission Creek.

As I climbed so did the mercury. I pulled out my umbrella and held it aloft. There was no tangible difference in temperature under my portable shade, but the intensity of the sun was diminished and for that alone I was grateful.

I felt a bit wobbly as I walked along the ridgetops between the two large river drainages, thousands of feet below. A familiar sucking sound indicated that I'd just drained the final drops of water from my hydration bladder. Thankfully, the trail had begun to descend.

The water of Mission Creek was reddish and long blooms of algae swayed in the shallow, warm flow. I grimaced, but I was desperate. Painstakingly, I filled one bottle and stuck in my SteriPEN. Once the UV light had sterilized the water, I poured it into my hydration bladder. I repeated the process until I'd treated three liters of water. Then, as a failsafe because I found the magic of UV too good to be true, I dropped a chlorine tablet in each bottle.

I consulted the water report I'd printed before I left home. Of the many crossings of Mission Creek over the next eighteen miles, three were reported to have had good water within the last two weeks. I hedged my bets on better water ahead and departed the algae-laden oasis.

As I worked my way up the twisted canyon, carved by Mission Creek's floods, I pondered how daily it was already sweltering when I awakened and how by noon the air shimmered with the heat. Even though no one was around to see me, I couldn't help but wonder: what would someone think of a woman walking alone across this austere landscape, clutching a silver umbrella? And what would they think about my clothes and body, caked in dirt, salt, and sunscreen, and stained by nosebleeds brought on by the arid climate?

I wasn't even sure what *I* thought of it.

I want to set a record because of the challenge. Is that really why I'm here? Or am I here because I need to thru-hike again, and the record is merely justification to repeat what most people call a once-in-a-lifetime experience?

Perhaps thru-hiking was the only way I could cope with modern life. Some people drank. Others used drugs. Some zoned out in front of the screen. My escape was the trail, where life was not easy or comfortable. It was longing for the life of a thru-hiker that had pulled me away from an otherwise comfortable and idyllic life on Bellingham Bay. My unhappiness with being a weekend warrior around a career and trips with my husband to the farmer's market had grown to unmanageable proportions.

I stepped across a mucky bit of ground thick with vibrant green grasses. In the back of my mind I had a nagging feeling. *This is the water source.* I dismissed it. The water report said the creek was flowing well. These muddy puddles were nothing.

A mile or so later the trail curved and dropped back to cross Mission Creek again. I was nearly out of water and ready to plop down and get more. My internal odometer told me that I'd traveled the right distance. I reached the edge of the creek bed and saw nothing but sand.

I stood in disbelief for several moments. The creek was bone dry.

BELLINGHAM, WASHINGTON / DECEMBER 2010

"I'm not making you happy anymore."

The words hung in the air above us as we lay in bed the morning after Christmas. I had nothing to say because I knew it was true. I wasn't happy. With myself. With anything. I couldn't find my way out of the depression that had been growing since we'd reached the end of our last thru-hike together four years before. I knew it wasn't his fault—or mine. I'd left Anish there along the Mexican border at the southern terminus of the Continental Divide Trail. Her voice called to me every day.

"Please. Can we not say divorce? Just . . . splitting up?" My voice seemed tiny in the space that had opened between us. Remy nodded.

Months later as we sat in the living room, now emptied of his half of our possessions, he asked me what it was that would make me happy again.

"What can you do to stop being depressed? What will you do now that I am gone?"

I sat there, too numb to verbalize. I picked up a notepad and pen and wrote the words that were a constant mantra in my mind: "I want to make hiking my life."

"How? How will you support yourself? Will you become a guide?"

"No. I don't know. I just can't do this anymore."

He was worried that I couldn't explain it or monetize it. He turned the notebook to a new page and wrote: Hikes I Want to Do.

I filled in a long list.

He labeled the top of the next page: Ways to Make Money Hiking.

I wrote guide and then crossed it out. Guiding was just as much of a cell as any other career. I didn't want to babysit. I wanted to walk my own path.

"I'll be poor and live in my tent year round. I'd rather be homeless and happy than anything else."

He sighed and closed the notebook. We were getting nowhere. Eventually he left.

DAY 8 (CONTINUED)

Each day on the trail I felt myself slipping a little farther into a primal state of mind, where all that mattered—all that existed—was surviving the day. I sought water and a safe place to sleep. I walked until I literally couldn't stand up because I was *driven*. Yet, I still had no idea what drove me, or where the drive came from. *Am I insane?* I preferred to believe that at least my escape was back in the direction from which humans had evolved. That somehow digression was superior to being dispassionate. But that drive, to be here, on the Pacific Crest Trail, attempting the record alone, had led to a dangerous crossroads. I pulled out my SPOT tracking beacon. I held it in my hand and opened the cover on the SOS button. All I had to do was push it and help would come. Local emergency personnel would receive my coordinates almost instantly. They would bring me fluids. Fly me to safety. I would sleep in a cool room and eat and drink until my body recovered. I wouldn't have to walk anymore. I could forget that I'd ever tried this.

"I might die of thirst out here," I said to the orange SPOT in my hand.

Tears rolled down my face. The moment of quitting I'd imagined on my first day hadn't been like this. It hadn't involved me sitting in the desert sun, dehydrated and dizzy, three miles down trail from the nearest water. I'd imagined simply being too tired or incapable of continuing. I had imagined being in control of my journey, even the end.

"Damn it, Anish, if you can cry then you are not too dehydrated to keep going!"

Angrily, I resecured the cover on the SOS button and put the SPOT device and my phone back in my pack. I rolled onto my hands and knees, coughing from the effort of speaking aloud with my dry throat.

"Get up. You haven't been through everything you've been through to quit because you're thirsty. It's three miles. Three fucking miles."

I heaved myself to my feet with great effort. "I might die out here, but I refuse to let it be today."

It was nearly 5 p.m. when I staggered into the parking area near the next water source. I looked around wild-eyed for the way to the spring. I knew it was a quarter of a mile off of the trail. A couple were just getting into their car.

"The spring?" I croaked. "Is it that way? Does it have water?"

"Yeah, follow the markers. You can't miss it." The man didn't seem to sense my urgency.

I hurried across a field and entered the woods. The temperature dropped noticeably as I entered a small cove of rock. Water, percolating through the soil above the stone grotto, dripped in a small but steady stream off of roots hanging down from the ceiling, pouring into an overflowing barrel.

I held my water bottle under the strongest drip and watched anxiously as it slowly filled. Giardia be damned, I chugged the liter of icy water. Then I filled and drank another. I pulled out my hydration bladder and began to fill it. My hands began to shake, and then the rest of me. I began to feel even more dizzy and then cold. Nausea threatened to empty me of the necessary fluids I'd just consumed. Shivering uncontrollably, I dropped the bladder and fumbled in my backpack for my sleeping bag. I draped it around my shoulders, leaned against the wall of rock with my eyes closed, and resumed filling the bladder.

I knew I was in shock from the sudden drop in temperature and the massive amount of cold water I'd consumed in a matter of seconds. I felt even dizzier now than when I'd been broiling in the sun. I noted the irony of feeling like I would die of heat for hours, and then moments later wrapping myself in a sleeping bag.

My vision started to go black. Screwing the lid onto my bladder, I just managed to stumble back to the sun-drenched field between the grotto and the trail before my legs buckled. I sat on the ground, unable to move for several minutes. In the depths of the canyon of Mission Creek, Death and I had again danced under a wicked sun. *How many more times will I be allowed to bow and walk away?* Finally, I got to my feet and headed north.

CHAPTER 8
SAN GORGONIO WILDERNESS, CALIFORNIA

DAY 8 (CONTINUED) / 44 MILES

It was several hours before I again achieved equilibrium in both body and mind. As night was falling, I realized that it was many, many miles to the next water and that I had taken only about half of what I needed from the spring. I wished I had gone back after I'd recovered from nearly passing out, rather than simply walking off in a daze with what I'd already collected. Resigned, I knew I would simply have to walk long into the night until I found water.

One of the quirkiest landmarks of the PCT is the housing of a variety of large stage animals at a private residence fifty yards off of the trail. In between their Hollywood performances, lions, tigers, bears and other animals watch hikers pass by from within their cages. I looked at the waypoints on my map and saw with apprehension that I was almost there. Emerging onto a network of dirt roads, I wound through a dark forest, feeling edgy. *What if one of the animals has escaped? What if this all ends with me getting eaten by a lion?*

I tried to calm myself by repeating over and over that I was being irrational. *These animals are in very strong cages. You're afraid of all kinds of irrational things like this when you're alone at night. Has anything ever happened? No. Now just keep walking.* I focused on the repetitive sound of my footsteps crunching on the gravel and the tiny spot of illuminated ground from my headlamp a few feet ahead. Just then, I heard a faint rustle to my right—a movement I didn't recognize. It was accompanied by a strong scent—not fecal matter or rotting carcasses—just the over-whelming odor of wild animal. I fought the rising panic that comes in the presence of an unseen predator by counting my breaths.

"Breathe 1, 2, 3 . . . breathe 1, 2, 3 . . . " I walked quickly, steadily. I felt eyes watching me—the eyes of instinctively curious nocturnal predators.

The road deteriorated into a two-track trail and soon the feeling of being watched dissipated. My breathing eased and the panicked feeling lessened. Still, I knew I had farther to travel before I'd be able to rest. I believed in the fences I couldn't see, but not completely.

Near midnight I crossed a rough jeep road. The moonlight illumi-nated three jugs of water alongside the trail. I bent down to examine them. They were full with a note that said, "For PCT hikers." If I'd had any energy at all I would have jumped for joy. Instead I unscrewed the cap off of one and drank half of it without stopping.

Five hours later my alarm woke me. I opened my eyes and realized I was lying in the road, curled around the half empty jug. I imagined myself crawling toward a gallon jug of water beneath circling vultures, only to find it empty. My throat made a croaking noise as I tried to talk myself into sitting upright. I would need to envision survival rather than demise if I was going to make it out of the desert.

CHAPTER 9
ANGELES NATIONAL FOREST, CALIFORNIA

DAY 9 / 39 MILES

I grabbed hold of the metal register stand on the summit of Mount Baden-Powell and tipped my head back. The indigo sky was littered with stars, indistinguishable from the dark desert, sprinkled with city lights, below. I felt as though I were afloat, in a space where they melded together. Only the feel of cold metal in my hands and the solid rock under my feet grounded me. It was 10 p.m. and I was breathless from running the quarter mile up the summit trail from the PCT. Slowly, I let go of the metal and threw my arms wide—embracing the night. I could not pass by this chance to stand on the mountain and touch the heavens. I spun around, the desert breeze billowing my dirty, torn skirt, before dashing back down to rejoin the PCT. I had already covered thirty-five miles that day and I had four more to travel before I could sleep.

DAY 10 / 40 MILES

Even though I'd passed through several large patches on my way up to Mount Baden-Powell the day before, I knew that the worst of the poodle dog bush was still to come. Visions of swollen, blistered skin and the threat of hospitalization bounced around in my brain like a pinball machine gone berserk. I could not stand the thought of giving up already, of losing this dream to a noxious weed. *You just survived a near miss with dehydration two days ago. A plant with a name like poodle dog is not going to end your hike.* I rounded the bend and found lush green slopes—poodle dog plants covered in purple, spike-like flowers. I picked up a stick from the ground and used it to gingerly push the plants aside. Weaving my way through was painstaking, but I was too focused to feel fear. I used many techniques to avoid the poodle dog: climbing above, sliding below, stepping on, gently prodding, and sucking in my gut as I skirted past. Eventually, I heard the gurgle of a spring and looked up from my intent focus. Ahead of me, a fox stood in the middle of the overgrown trail—staring.

"Hey there, handsome one." At the sound of my voice, he dashed through the plants I was struggling to avoid—disappearing down a gully. He was gone so fast I wondered if he'd even been there. I realized I was shaking from the repressed fear.

I gathered some water from the spring, took a deep breath to collect myself, and continued on. Progress was achingly slow. Finally, I reached open grassy slopes beneath a stand of trees, both burned and living. I breathed for what felt like the first time in hours. Having passed through the poodle dog bushes unscathed, I felt like the Israelites as they emerged from the Red Sea. I hurled the stick into the forest and sped up. I had begun my traverse of the overgrown slopes when the sun was high in the sky. Now it was sinking and I felt the pressure of lost time and the miles I had to make up. For the past hour I had been so focused that I had lost track of everything except my proximity to the harmful plants. Now, free of that focus, I faced only the day's remaining distance—twelve more miles. Awareness of my aching body and throbbing feet came rushing back. I soon found myself engulfed in tears.

"God, I can't do this. It's too hard. I'm so scared of getting a poodle dog rash. Of infections. Waterborne illness. The heat. I might die of dehydration. I hurt. I hurt so much that I can't sleep. I can't even eat. It's all too much."

I felt the vast impossibility of what I was attempting swell in my mind. Hiking twenty-six hundred miles in two months was incomprehensible when I thought about the whole. Each morning, even the forty or so miles I needed to walk boggled my mind. I did not want to be miserable for the entirety of the trail. I was only ten days into this and I hadn't had so much as one twinge-free moment. Even now as the golden light of day bathed the forest, I was distracted by the difficulties and fear. I placed my hand on the blackened bark of a burned—yet living—pine tree and bawled.

A pink and silver butterfly fluttered to-and-fro anxiously near my feet. Two hands scooped it up, but did not crush it. Instead, they cradled it gently as it banged around, flapping desperately. I heard a quiet voice speak, "Little butterfly." The hands opened to the sun, revealing a perched butterfly inside. Though the wings were still, the body was heaving as though it could barely breathe.

"Little butterfly. Don't you trust me? I will take care of everything." The heaving slowed and for a moment the butterfly was at rest. "There now. I will take care of you. OK? There is just one thing you must do. You know what that is."

The butterfly crawled onto the fingers and looked over the edge. It nodded, and whispered, "Just walk."

"Yes, just walk."

The butterfly launched into the air and disappeared.

I looked around, confused. I was alone, and yet I had seen and heard everything as clear as day. *Am I going crazy? Or was it a vision sent from another realm?* I felt as though it was a mix of both things, but I didn't care. Something more than the sunset light surrounded me—rather, it radiated from inside of me. I felt infused with peace. A calmness and a strength that I had never felt before was glowing in my soul. I spoke to the silent forest around me. "Just walk, Anish, just walk."

I heard a cracking noise below me. I looked down into the burned forest below. Perched in a snag I saw the powerful body of a bear ripping the tree apart. Pieces crashed into the forest as he sought out his dinner. I smiled and walked into the dusk.

Hours later, I arrived at a remote fire station. It was just after midnight. As I lay in my tent waiting for sleep to come, I realized that it was my tenth day on the trail and that I had averaged 41.9 miles per day. Trying to ignore my throbbing, aching body, I felt very aware of every last brutal second of those 419 trail miles. Yet, there was something else I was now aware of, something that hadn't been there before. The vision from the trail that afternoon had left me unafraid.

DAY 11 / 34 MILES

My nose was bleeding . . . again. Just as it had every afternoon for the last week. Big, red drops pummeled the dust as I walked. I hardly even noticed anymore. I simply tried to hold my face at an angle to keep the blood from staining my white shirt. The buzzing and shimmering of the superheated air grew in intensity, making me feel dizzy. The sun was high and the trail wound through a labyrinth of endless canyons. I felt more than ever that I was wandering aimlessly through the desert. I fought to remain focused on my goal for the day—Agua Dulce—and the goal of the entire journey. I could still feel the residue of my brush with death in Mission Creek clinging to my psyche. *And what of yesterday's visions?* I began to understand how one could be literally driven insane from heat and sun exposure.

At long last, I spotted the highway far below. I looked back at the winding route I'd followed upward through the stifling canyons, and then forward. I whispered the words that flowed into my mind along with the fresh air at the top of the ridge, "As false summits are to mountain ridges, so too are the kinks and bends of a canyon. With each, what was hidden is revealed—the world is recreated right before your eyes."

Recreated it was. From wandering in a remote, barren desert to the vista of a busy highway in a matter of minutes. I knew that from the pavement it was only ten miles of trail to the small town of Agua Dulce. A mere ten miles to ice cream and food and laundry and a hug from Donna Saufley at Hiker Heaven—the most famous trail angel along the Pacific Crest Trail. New socks would be waiting for me there, as long as REI had indeed overnighted the order I'd made from my phone. For the last four days I had been hiking in nothing but holey rags that barely protected my ravaged feet. The increased friction meant my blisters now bulged to seemingly impossible sizes—each nearly a half-inch thick. My only comfort was that they were still filled with clear fluid—no sign of an infection . . . yet.

I reached the highway and checked the Halfmile app. The PCT veered left and then climbed up and over some more ridges before reaching Agua Dulce. To the right it was only two-tenths of a mile to a KOA campground. There would be ice cold beverages and air conditioning . . . I could not help myself. My feet turned right and flew across the sandy field.

Cooled and refreshed by Gatorade and ten minutes inside an air-conditioned building, I rejoined the PCT. Although I was somewhat annoyed at myself for giving into the temptation, I couldn't be too angry. I was again climbing beneath the burning sun. The loss of a half hour was well worth it.

The Antelope Valley Freeway was visible from an agonizingly far distance away. When I at last reached the culvert where the PCT passes beneath the road, I was appalled by how long it had taken me to get there. I was moving at one mile per hour rather than my normal two to three. It seemed as though the entirety of the last two days had taken place in slow motion and an otherworldly haze.

The long culvert dumped me into the maze of unmarked trails inside the faulted, honeycombed red rocks of Vasquez Rocks Natural Area Park. I tried to stay on the main path but, when I consulted the app, found I was a quarter mile off-trail—climbing eastward and away from the PCT. I turned around and headed down again, this time using my app to pick the correct canyon.

I verified every junction until I at last crested the climb and saw a paved highway ahead of me. With renewed vigor I plowed down the road, reaching the large Sweetwater general store in short order. I threw my pack into the cart and wandered around, overwhelmed by the options. The complexity of shopping was far more difficult than opening a box and putting the contents in my pack, especially with my brain still in a muddled state after hours in the unforgiving sun. It took far longer than I wished to decide on what I needed for a day and a half of hiking and what I wanted to eat for dinner that night. I was glad that this was the only time on the trail that I had planned to buy anything. At last I found myself wrapping a pint of ice cream in my sleeping bag so it wouldn't melt on the way to the Saufley's, a mile off of the trail. Twenty minutes later I saw the familiar fence outside Hiker Heaven.

Stepping through the gate marked with a PCT emblem, I experienced the incredible sense of peace that always hung about the Saufleys. Large tents full of cots were set up on the lawn, along with a few trailers of varying size. Hikers milled around a large campfire pit at the center of the space. A herd of small dogs bounded toward me, barking a greeting I was certain they delivered to every hiker that came through. The other hikers and the handful of volunteers looked at me. I suddenly felt conspicuous, tentative, shy. Being around people had always been stressful for me and more so now, after days of solitude in the desert. I hadn't seen Jeff and Donna Saufley since 2005, but as I scanned the faces turned my way I recognized Jeff's face immediately. A little less hair than last time, but still Jeff. He greeted me warmly and I felt my anxiety lessen, reassured that this was a safe place full of love for wayfaring hikers.

"You can borrow clothes from that rack. And here's a laundry basket for your dirty things. Donna will wash everything for you. I think the trailer has an empty room and there shouldn't be a line for a shower," Jeff was reciting the Hiker Heaven instructions without sounding robotic.

I smiled. He didn't remember me. But then again, they saw hundreds of hikers every year. No doubt several thousand filthy, stinky women had passed through since the last time I'd been here. I set my pack down and pulled clean clothes from the hangers. I was so very ready for laundry and a shower. I greeted a couple of other hikers and helpers who were lounging in lawn chairs.

Donna appeared from inside the house. "We've been waiting for you!"

She enveloped me in a hug and I immediately forgot the *absolute everything* of the last ten days. For at least the next few hours, I would not have to endure hardship.

"Are you the Ghost?!" a hiker nearby asked.

I looked at him, confused. "No, I'm Anish."

"But you're trying to set the record, right?"

"Yes . . . " I stood there for a second trying to figure out who the Ghost was and how it related to me.

Donna intervened by herding me toward the trailer and away from the curious rounds of questions, now coming from all directions. I blissfully showered and returned to the circle of lawn chairs and light near the garage. Donna handed me a small package from REI and took my laundry. I sank to the pavement with my bowl of salad and several pairs of new socks. There were two young men there who were obviously thru-hiking. The unkempt beards and the Saufley Electric shirts from the rack were dead giveaways.

"Is that all you're going to eat?!" Jeff asked.

"Vegetables are all I want right now."

"Here's a chair," an older man, whom I'd surmised was a volunteer, offered.

"No, thanks. I'm fine on the ground."

I sat there answering questions and allowing myself to just rest. This would probably be the only time I'd stop at 7 p.m. the entire journey.

"How far do you walk every day?"

"About forty miles."

"It's been hotter than hell. I can't imagine hiking that far in it," the hiker who'd asked me if I was the Ghost said.

I went back to the trailer to get the ice cream which I had tucked into the freezer. As I walked back, I noticed that my bare feet rolled smoothly along the flagstones. I felt a quiver of excitement in my gut. This was the first glimmer of hope that my body could adapt to the rigorous demands I was placing on it. The sense of peace and reassurance I had experienced the day before sparkled in my soul. I returned to the circle, ice cream in hand, and took the offered chair.

"Ice cream, now we're talking! You need calories!" someone said.

"Who is the Ghost?" I asked.

There was silence for a few moments as people looked back and forth. "You."

I wasn't sure who said it, but I could tell from the looks on their faces that it was true.

The dryer dinged and Donna handed me my clean, warm clothes. My whole body craved sleep. I mumbled thank you and goodbye and stood to leave. Donna rose as well and said, "I better say goodbye now, because you're probably going to be out of here stupid early."

She wrapped me in another hug and said quietly, "I have never cheered for someone to break Scott's record before, but I want you to. Go get 'em girl!"

I fell asleep with her words ringing in my ears. They would be a source of strength to pull me through some of the darkest times of the next fifty days.

CHAPTER 10
MOJAVE DESERT, CALIFORNIA

DAY 12 / 44 MILES

The morning was cold and bathed in soft yellow light. The desert landscape was an impressionist vision—muted earth tones blended from desert floor to high country. I followed a meandering desert ridgeline toward the flat, empty expanse of the Mojave crossing. In the far distance the blue humps of the Tehachapi Mountains rose up out of the vastness like a line of tortoises marching across the horizon. I reached the hostel called Hikertown very early and picked up my resupply box from the owner, which included my first change of shoes. I slipped my battered feet into the fresh trail runners and headed out—walking on new-shoe marshmallow clouds. More than five hundred miles now lay behind me.

The aqueduct walk was just as I had remembered it: flat, windswept, and sandy. After only a few miles the route turned away from the open canal of the California Aqueduct and began to follow the Los Angeles Aqueduct pipeline. The heat and the dry air made me thirsty. Thousands of inaccessible gallons of water flowed through the pipe I walked along. Its presence messed with my mind. So I powered along the dirt roads, trying to keep my mind occupied with thoughts of anything and everything else. I thought of my ex and how he would soon be starting his own thru-hike in the opposite direction. I thought about our good-natured bet on who would make it to the Columbia River first. I pulled my phone out of my pocket and turned it on: full service.

"Hello?" Remy's voice was a mix of concern and curiosity. "Are you OK?"

"I'm fine. Just walking across the aqueduct. Boring. You remember."

"Yeah, I do," he chuckled.

"Hey, so, I just wanted to call and say congratulations. Graduation is this weekend, right?"

"Yes. Thank you. I just got my finals back. Going to graduate *summa cum laude*. My parents are flying in today actually. I need to leave soon to pick them up."

"That's wonderful. Congratulations. I never had any doubt that you would. When are you beginning your hike?"

"Next week. I'm going to a wedding on the Fourth of July, so I will get off trail for three days and then back on. You might be able to beat me to the Columbia with that little advantage."

I laughed and he did too. We talked for a couple of minutes before he had to leave to pick up his parents. I turned my phone off and slid it back into my pack.

A few minutes later a pickup rumbled to a stop. The men inside offered me a beer, which I declined. They chatted with me for a while, but I just wanted to keep moving. To get the hell out of this place. In passing, they mentioned a man just ahead of me. After they drove off I walked faster, eager to meet my first thru-hiker of the day on trail.

In the desert—where the flat horizon enables you to see incredibly far—things come into view instantly, as though transported from another plane. The other hiker appeared in just this way. I walked faster than ever, eager to converse with a new hiker. As I drew closer, I saw him look back multiple times.

When I finally reached him, I said hello.

He greeted me with, "Are you Snorkel?"

"No, I'm Anish."

"Oh. I thought you were the woman trying to set the speed record."

"I am."

First the Ghost and now Snorkel . . . would anyone ever know that it was Anish who moved through the landscape forty miles a day with everything she needed to survive on her back? Or would I remain forever anonymous . . . a whispered legend along the trail? I realized that I might prefer that perception to one of fame—so that I might walk alone forever.

We fell into stride. It felt fulfilling to walk with someone moving my pace, taking my mind off of my blisters, the sun, the flat roads—the twenty-one hundred miles between myself and Canada.

"Any idea where Snorkel is?" I asked him. "I saw her name in a register ages ago."

"I heard she got off of the trail. But then, I didn't think there was anyone on trail behind me, so I was confused when I saw you gaining so fast."

"Oh. Hmm. Do you know who the Ghost is?" I wondered if he'd have any more information for me.

"No. Never heard of them."

"Oh."

We walked in silence for a while. I knew who Snorkel was from mutual friends. She was a well-known hiker and many people were aware of her attempt at the FKT. I'd found out about it just days before I'd flown to San Diego when a friend had texted me a screenshot of her Facebook announcement. I understood this hiker's confusion. After all, I was no one—an eidolon. Even though he was friendly, just like the hikers at the Saufley's, I couldn't help but feel that I was under scrutiny. I'd scoured pictures of Snorkel after I'd gotten that text. She was thin. She had a shoe sponsor. She held the self-supported record on the Appalachian Trail. She was everything I wasn't. If someone was supposed to break this record, it was her. *Did my newfound companion believe me? Would anyone believe me? Did it matter to me if anyone believed me? Who was the Ghost? Was it really me? If it is, where on earth did someone come up with it? Or is there another woman somewhere in this desert moving fast toward Canada?*

We parted ways at Cottonwood Creek and I continued up into the Tehachapi Mountains. There was a debilitating headwind, and I could feel my energy being depleted by my battle with it along with the steep ravines. I crested a ridge and found myself leaning heavily into the wind. For several long seconds I was suspended, all my weight resting on an invisible force. I was keenly aware of the entirety of the world around me—of discomfort and fatigue, wind and sun, waning daylight and impending darkness. At last gravity won, my lifted knee driving downward, my planted foot leaving the sand. Moving again, I felt the warm wetness and instantaneous relief that signaled a bursting blister. I plummeted downward and up the next slope, relishing the release. Now began the long road of keeping a burst blister infection-free.

CHAPTER 11
TEHACHAPI MOUNTAINS, CALIFORNIA

DAY 12 (CONTINUED) / 44 MILES

Finally, I escaped the fifty-mile-per-hour winds of the open desert floor and found respite in Tylerhorse Canyon. My throat was sandpaper from the wind as I hurried toward the water that flowed into the ravine. I fell on my knees as I reached the creek, eager to splash my face. In the twilight I was able to see that while, yes, it had water—the merest trickle—it was thick with red algae. I sat back on my heels, devastated. I could comb the water more effectively than scoop it into my bottle. I knew that I was almost out, having carried little from Cottonwood Creek in hopes of filling up here. I was disgusted with myself for allowing my balking at water weight to imperil me. I'd been spoiled by front-country water access for a few days and let my guard down. I needed to remember that there were no faucets up ahead.

Night was falling and, with it, the temperatures. For once the elements were working in my favor. I decided to bypass the disgusting creek and night hike across the Tehachapi Mountains to where water flowed on the far side of the range. Onward I climbed—leaving the protected canyon—back into the ferocious gale. Now that the sun had retired from its brutal throne, the wind had become wicked enough to throw me off balance and slice into flesh with freezing precision—even though I had put on a wind shirt. As the moon rose overhead, I was thankful to have its light augmenting my wan headlamp. I had forgotten to include batteries in the box I'd mailed to Hikertown and there were none to buy there. I would be in total darkness once this set died completely. It was a nearly unforgivable omission on my part, but I had to let it go. Release it to the currents of air swirling past.

The trail wound through canyon after canyon, traveling up and over ridges in between. Every time I thought I saw the top, the trail would curve, meander, and again climb. My weary mind began to insist that there was no end.

"Is this climb ever going to end?" I shouted to hear my own self over the howling wind.

You'll never reach the top tonight. This terrain is too difficult. You're too tired to fight the wind anymore.

"I have to. I have to get to water." I verbally fought back against the rising desperation my thoughts had brought out. The Sisyphean route coupled with the battle against the wind left me ragged in mind and body.

The light of my headlamp illuminated a few jugs of water cached alongside the trail. I wondered who put them there. In the confusing maze of ups and downs, I'd lost all sense of where I was. I collapsed into a ball next to a crate of water bottles near the jugs. I pulled my sleeping bag out of my pack and huddled in it. I mechanically chewed and swallowed some dried fruit, washing it down with a bottle of water. A mouse approached me, hopeful for some crumbs, while staying just beyond my reach. It needn't have worried, I was too exhausted to spare energy for shooing it away. I knew that I could not stay there—even though I was sorely tempted. I was still three miles from my anticipated campsite. I packed up my things and walked onward.

At last I felt as though I had actually crossed to the other side of the range. My watch beeped, reminding me to eat. I ignored its prompt, but glanced at the time—10 p.m. I switchbacked downward through burned-out forest, wracking my memory vault for what this place had looked like eight years before. In the midst of trying to recall the past, a pair of eyes reflected in my headlamp just a few feet ahead, catching me off guard.

I stopped, momentarily confused as my fatigued brain attempted to process this new information. Large, yellow cat eyes blinked at me as I held my headlamp aloft. My mind quickly searched for everything I knew about nocturnal felines, encouraged by the proximity of a large predator: Raise your hands. Yell. Try to scare it off.

I clicked my headlamp to its strobe setting, raised my hands, and waved them above my head. I was surprised to hear the guttural, menacing sound of a large dog barking nearby. Combined with my lightshow and flailing antics, it prompted the mountain lion to move a few feet up the hill. It paused there and looked at me again. It was then that I realized that *I* was the one barking. With a surge of confidence at its apparent effectiveness, I barked again—the sounds echoing from deep in my belly. With one more glance back at me, the mountain lion ran uphill—disappearing into the windy darkness.

Fueled by adrenaline, I hiked faster than I had since that morning. Every few minutes I glanced back, scanning the terrain with my headlamp. After three checks with no feline results, I relaxed. I was not being followed.

I arrived at my planned camp shortly after seeing the lion, but I hadn't anticipated an extensive burn or a large predator there, so I continued on. Another mile or two passed before I found a slightly sloped piece of ground that was not beneath a burned snag that might break from the winds and fall on me in the night. The bottle of water I'd carried from the cache was still in my pack—I had forgotten to drink in the excitement of the cougar encounter. It was enough to allow me to camp now that I'd finally found a suitable home for the night. I'd reach the creek near the road in the morning.

I set up my tent while giggling to myself, remembering the words of a jovial Hawaiian man at a trailhead on Kauai years ago: "We hunt wild boars with dogs. If you hear a boar, bark at it. Scares them away." Though I'd laughed at the time, thinking the advice was meant to embarrass *haoles*, my Rottweiler impression had now proven effective against not only feral pigs on Maui, where I'd convinced even my hiking partner that I was a big dog, but also Tehachapi mountain lions.

As I stretched out in my bag, I noticed that my legs ached less. Hot needles still shot along my left sciatic nerve, from piriformis to ankle, while I walked, but it was no longer enough to keep me awake. I slid my hand along my stomach. When I'd weighed myself at Hiker Heaven I was ten pounds less than my start weight. At that rate I would lose another fifty pounds, which was certainly not possible. I reassured myself that it was mostly water and that I'd be fine. But I knew that the math definitely didn't add up. I was still barely capable of taking in two thousand calories a day. My body was dipping deeply into its stores, and I'd only be able to borrow from that bank for so long. My last conscious thought was hoping that fifty more days wasn't too much to ask.

CHAPTER 12

PIUTE MOUNTAINS, CALIFORNIA

DAY 13 / 42 MILES

Sometimes the difference between night and day is greater than the contrast between light and dark. In the morning I was less focused on the hardships of the hike. The wind continued to buffet me as I followed the trail down into a deep valley, but it was now a friendly, cooling force. The daily routine had begun to soothe me in the way that only order and exertion could. Under the morning sunshine, less intense than its afternoon counterpart, I felt the joy of hiking bubbling up and overflowing inside me, overcoming even the aching in my feet. Over the past few days I'd begun to think about food often, yet my stomach still refused to accept it. My watch beeped and I ate a cookie. I gagged on it, but managed to swallow.

I thought about how the night before I had faced one of my greatest fears, and with an unexpected nonchalance. I felt empowered by my encounter with the mountain lion, even though I half-wondered if I'd imagined it. My deep—albeit short lived—sleep between the stand-off and the present moment left my brain feeling hazy. I was finding that the amount of rest I got each night had a direct bearing on my ability to focus and think clearly the next day. Yet, I was positive that it had been real.

By midday a second blister had popped. I knew I must be careful to apply triple antibiotic cream to both of them now—morning and night. I'd seen what an infected blister could do to a person's body and knew it would end my hike if I allowed it to happen to me. All day my thoughts revolved around the scenery, the cougar, any type of food other than what was on my back, and how to keep my blisters free of bacteria.

I fought to keep the image of Rabbit out of my mind. In 2005 he'd come into the Vermilion Valley Resort in the heart of the Sierra with an infected blister. His eyes were glassy, his skin was flushed, and a feverish sweat clung to him. He didn't even seem to recognize us.

We saw him again much later. He'd ended up hospitalized and so far behind the pack of hikers that he headed to the Canadian border, hiking south in an attempt to get back to Vermilion Valley before snow fell. He didn't make it. If my blisters developed infections, it could be catastrophic for my hike—not to mention the record attempt.

Despite how good I felt, the last ten miles of the day were agonizing, as they always were. Pushing beyond the thirty-mile mark always seemed to signal the breakdown of my body and a downward spiral in my attitude. The order was predictable by mile. First the stabbing in my sciatic nerve started shortly after mile thirty-three. By mile thirty-five my feet were throbbing. Finally, forty miles into my day, the accumulated fatigue made me feel as though I was wading through mud. Depending on how long it took me to reach my predetermined campsite each night, I often walked the final mile or two with tears of desperation rolling down my face.

Yet I stayed staunchly devoted to the schedule I'd made before I left home. Long ago—sitting on a sunny lawn at a friend's home—I'd marked my stack of printed maps with each night's campsite. It had been so easy to measure out forty or so miles and mark little tent symbols on the level areas of the contour lines. On the trail, putting in the effort required to reach those plotted points was far more difficult. I clung to the hope that someday my body would not ache. That it would cover the miles easily and accept food joyfully. I daydreamed of being anything but thirsty and hot, longing to reach the polished granite and glistening lakes of the High Sierra.

"I refuse to let this suffering be for nothing. In fact, I refuse to suffer," I whispered to myself as I pushed each tent stake into the ground. "I can adapt. I am adapting. I will adapt." Another long day was done and I was forty-two miles closer to Canada.

The trail diverged from the dirt road that it had been following through scrubland and scraggly pine forest. A short while later I veered west onto a spur trail that led to Robin Bird Spring. My expectations of reliable water had been annihilated after so many false hopes over the preceding week and a half. I expected to find yet another dry basin where water used to be.

Instead I found cold water gushing from a pipe. It startled me so much that I stared for a long minute. Then, I dropped to the ground and began to drink and fill, drink and fill. The climb into the Piute Mountains had proven challenging even though the trail was in good condition. I had been mostly going uphill since the night before and the morning had quickly given way to crushing heat. When I awoke that morning, my mouth and throat were unable to create sound—I had felt mummified. Daily, my urine—when I managed to pee, which wasn't often—was a dark orange. By the time I found myself at the oasis of Robin Bird Spring, I'd already traveled eighteen waterless miles since the previous water source the night before. From there, it was going to be thirty-five miles to the turnoff to Yellow Jacket Spring—plus an additional one and a half miles round-trip from the trail. I stopped thinking and drank some more.

I heaved myself onto my feet. The hottest part of the day was imminent. I needed to move. Within a short time, I departed the scraggly forest and entered a landscape of sand and yucca. The six liters of water on my back worked in synergy with the triple-digit heat to physically weigh me down until my walk became a shuffle. The new landscape in front of me was an expanse of emptiness. A lonesomeness—the type that only the desert can make you feel—crept over me.

"This must be what walking through hell is like." My voice was hoarse, but I needed to speak. I needed conversation, even if it was with myself.

I crossed dirt roads that led down canyons and cut across hillsides.

"Who comes here? Why?" I coughed with the effort of coaxing words from my parched throat.

In a small parking area, I encountered an interpretive sign that the incessant UV radiation had rendered only faintly visible. A good reminder to smear some more sunscreen on my exposed skin. While I did so, I read about the desert tortoise. Turning away from the bleached placard and continuing the climb into the Piutes, I couldn't help but feel that my plodding was akin to that of the tortoise. According to the sign, they were able to survive temperatures of up to 140 degrees and go a year without drinking water. Unlike me, they were the epitome of desert efficiency.

I reached the junction of rough dirt roads at Bird Spring Pass very late in the afternoon—much faster than my reptilian counterpart could have. Surprisingly, a few gallon jugs of water were tied together and secured to one of a handful of Joshua trees—the only vegetation in sight. I propped my umbrella up on the branches and sat beneath it. I investigated the water report and examined my own unconsumed stock. Happily, I discovered that I'd been more efficient than I'd thought. Perhaps I was not as efficient as a tortoise, but I still had plenty of water to travel to Yellow Jacket Spring—perhaps even farther to McIvers Spring. I scoured the information on each source as well as scrutinized the dates they'd last been updated on the now-crumpled water report. I vowed not to let a repeat of the Mission Creek snafu happen to me again and had printed out a more up-to-date version at Hiker Heaven.

This revised set of updates was only two weeks old. That meant I had already gained a month on some of the hikers ahead of me. My cracked lips hurt as I smiled. I wasn't racing them, but it seemed like the only tangible measure of my progress. Alone, I had nothing to compare myself to except myself—and the damnable stack of maps merrily stating how far I would walk each day. Even though I was reaching those locations without fail, the milestones seemed to float without a reference point. *I'm moving twice as fast as other hikers. Twice as fast as I did last time. Last time it took me over four months. Half that is a little over two. Will I be able to keep this up? Do I need to move even faster? I don't think I can, but I am feeling stronger.* I was demanding the impossible from my body every day with hardly any chance for recovery—and I was beginning to feel that it was rallying to the challenge.

I leaned back on my elbows in the tiny puddle of shade cast by the umbrella. Distantly I heard an engine. To my surprise, I saw clouds of dust down in the canyon—people were riding ATVs.

"So that's who comes here."

I got up and hiked onward, eagerly anticipating the moment when the sun would drop behind the first ridge and I'd begin to walk in shadows— by far my favorite part of every day. The protracted climbs and descents across the Piutes were no different than all the other miles I'd traveled since Campo on day one. Yet, as I crested a ridgeline near evening I realized that I hadn't even thought about the switchbacking incline. Instead I'd been watching the moon rise over a blushing horizon and the bats near to me fluttering through the cooling air. I paused and slipped my windbreaker on, chilled now that the sun was gone.

I'm adapting.

Night fell softly and I inhaled the sweet smell of the desert. It was an unmistakable earthy scent—dry with hints of floral and creosote floating on minute breezes. I descended into a lowland where golden oaks, soaring into the inky sky, indicated the concealed presence of water beneath the ground. I had reached my tent symbol for today. Searching amid the leaves and hummocks of brown earth, I found a flat area to nestle down. I pitched my tent and stretched out my beaten body. There were no spasms. It felt sublime to fully relax into the arms of Mother Earth beneath the gaze of Sister Moon.

DAY 15 / 46 MILES

At Walker Pass, along California Route 178, I met two men who were thru-hiking. They were standing at the edge of the road, thumbs out, waiting for a ride.

"Hi. Heading into Onyx?"

"No, Lake Isabella," said the man with a stained red shirt as yet another car roared by.

The other guy, with a huge blonde beard, sat down on his pack, keeping his face turned away from me and toward oncoming traffic.

"OK. Well, good luck." I turned and embarked on the merciless ascent up from Walker Pass.

The encounter with them brought my thru-hiker tally to ten since departing Hiker Heaven. The two men at the road were obviously not interested in talking to me, even though I was desperate for interaction.

Each time I met another hiker I stopped to talk, excited. It was awkward at first to engage my vocal chords, and even more awkward to carry on a conversation with another human. I often felt as though I'd been in a monastic silence for years rather than mere days.

Eventually the grade eased and I began to follow a ridgeline. Unlike the steep climb, the ridgeline was partially shaded. Happy to have reached an elevation where bona fide trees grew, sheltering the top of my head, I leaned my umbrella on my shoulder to block the sunlight coming from behind me. Ahead I could see where the trail passed through a narrow gap in the ridge. To my surprise, there was a woman resting in it. I increased my pace slightly, motivated by the potential of meeting another female thru-hiker.

It was obvious as soon as I arrived at the gap that she was out for a day hike. Her tiny pack was open beside her while she nibbled on a sandwich. My stomach growled.

"Hello," I said, happy for an excuse to stop walking. Perhaps she'd be more interested in talking.

"Hi," she said, taking a bite of sandwich.

I tried not to stare at her snacks. "Are you thru-hiking?"

"No. Are you?"

"Yes." I'd already known her answer, but I was at a loss for anything else to say.

"Nice day," she said.

I nodded and turned away. "Enjoy."

My watch beeped, indicating that an hour had passed and it was time to try and force myself to eat again. Reaching into the pocket of my pack, I absently pulled out a bar, tore it open, and took a bite. Then another, and another. I crumpled the empty wrapper and stuck it back into my pocket. My stomach growled again. *I'm hungry!*

I wanted to shout with the excitement of it. Though it was a primal instinct, hunger had eluded me for fifteen days. This was a pivotal moment. Now—despite the heat, fatigue, and extreme effort—my body was no longer shunning food. I pulled out a baggie of Oreos and devoured them. Then a baggie of crackers.

"OK, Anish," I told myself, "you have to stop or you'll run out of food before you get to Kennedy Meadows."

CHAPTER 13
OWENS PEAK WILDERNESS, CALIFORNIA

DAY 16 / 43 MILES

I feel like a cat on a perch, stalking the roof of the world. The thought floated through my mind as I crossed the shoulder of the high point of the ridge—Spanish Needle—in mellow afternoon light. Its granitic summit protruded into the sky a short distance away, while a beautiful desert canyon sprawled below me with a trail visibly winding through it. For once, everything was perfect and blissful. I spread my arms wide and ran down the trail. I was light, free, and happy. My heart was brimming with joy. I would reach Kennedy Meadows the next day. The desert would be behind me and I would ascend to the grand heights of the High Sierra. There, bare, gray rock formations soared above lush, green valleys. Snow clung to the highest crags and crystal-clear rivers gushed across the land. I looked forward to following the much more established John Muir Trail for nearly two hundred miles across the sublime alpine landscapes.

The top of the world feeling ended as I stopped to get some water at a river crossing along a dirt road a few miles later. Hungry, I looked inside my nearly empty pack and was at once thankful and dismayed. Truly ravenous hiker hunger had hit me, for which I was immensely grateful. Yet, I'd plowed through my meager supply at triple the speed I had been eating and was down to just three bars with over thirty miles to go to reach my resupply box.

Cool air settled around me as I walked from late afternoon into evening. I ate sparingly, but it was hard to ignore the hunger stabbing my gut. Darkness fell hours before I would reach my intended campsite and my water ran out when I was still two miles from the next spring. It was all exactly as it had been for the last sixteen days—a roller coaster, but at last I felt like I could predict the undulations of the ride.

I reached the turnoff to the next spring and went a short ways downhill to reach it. A metal trough was catching a trickle of water from a pipe. By headlamp, I investigated the water pooled in the trough. It was thick with algae, so I propped my bottle under the dripping pipe and leaned back on my pack. I turned off my headlamp and gazed at the cold, bright stars. I spotted the Big Dipper and noted where Cassiopeia was in her continuous dance around the Polaris.

The sound of the water piling up in my bottle changed tone, alerting me that it was full. I used my SteriPEN to sterilize the water and then poured it into my hydration bladder. Once again, I propped the empty bottle under the flow and leaned back. My heat-attuned body went from chilled to violently shivering in a matter of seconds. It was anomalous and frightening after so much heat. I dug my sleeping bag out of my pack and crawled into it with my shoes still on. My teeth chattered together loudly—so much so that they drowned out the sound of the water. After a few minutes I warmed enough to stop shivering. Once again, I sterilized the water and set the bottle in place for a third time.

As I again rested my head on my pack, I thought to myself that this was likely to be a very bad idea. My eyelids were so heavy. I tried to focus on the sound of the water, listening for the change in pitch that would indicate it was time to sit up.

I lurched awake, uncertain of how long I'd been asleep. I turned on my headlamp and looked at my bottle. It was overflowing onto the hardpacked dirt. I grabbed it and hastily used the SteriPEN.

"How could you fall asleep? You knew it was a bad idea." I berated myself aloud as I poured the water into my hydration bladder and packed away my sleeping bag.

"Ten p.m. For God's sake, you were asleep for an hour."

Disgusted with myself, I hurried through the cold night, shivering until the energy emanating from my own muscles warmed me. *I need to go at least another five miles. I'll be walking until midnight!* Self-directed anger fueled me for the next forty-five minutes. By 11 p.m. I'd run into a wall—a wall built from fatigue and hunger. My fast walk downshifted into a stumble and then I fell down. I got up and continued onward, but soon I had to admit defeat. Too exhausted to walk anymore, I pitched my tent right on the trail and crawled inside. It wasn't hard to convince myself to skip dinner in order to ration my food because I was too tired to eat anyway.

DAY 17 / 35 MILES

The sound of my watch combined with intense pangs of hunger rousted me from my deep sleep. It was difficult to remember where I was and why. I began to pack up, pointedly ignoring my stomach. There was one bar in my food bag and I was twenty-one miles from Kennedy Meadows, the last resupply point before the High Sierra.

I walked through the high desert terrain, directing my attention to the sagebrush, chaparral, and anything I could think of—anything but hunger. I imagined the alpine landscape that lay just ahead of me. *The Sierra Nevada—Range of Light—a beacon to me. The promised land after the desert; replete with sparkling water, snowcapped peaks, and valleys riddled with bears. Be still my heart, we're almost home.*

"Be still and don't think about food," I added wryly to my poetic thoughts.

Hourly, my watch beeped reminding me to eat. Each time I took one small bite from the bar I had left—seven bites rationed across seven hours.

My mind swam with hunger. It took colossal effort to quell its primal raging and do some math instead. I was only seventeen days deep into the hike, about to cross the seven-hundred-mile mark. *Maybe I did have what it took?* I had so far. I calculated carefully what lie ahead. *If I can manage to maintain a forty-mile-per-day average through the next two hundred or so miles of the High Sierra—arguably the most physically demanding portion of the entire PCT—then I will reach Tuolumne Meadows by Sunday night, or maybe Monday. If I can manage that, then I will reach the one-thousand-mile mark eleven days from now. If I keep the same pace, I'll reach Echo Lake by the Fourth of July.*

If . . . if . . . if . . .

There were so many ifs. In fact, the entire journey seemed to be nothing more than a string of fragile *if*s held together by a glue stick of stubbornness, like the paper chains I'd made as a child to adorn our Christmas tree. A festoon of *if water is there*s and *if I can just keep moving*s, alternating with the *if I don't die of dehydration*s and the *if only I can stay strong and determined enough*s, formed a bright garland of memories trailing behind me. They seemed flimsy in my retrospective scrutiny. In fact, I was surprised that the adhesive—my own stubborn nature—hadn't disintegrated under the implacable radiation of the desert sun.

Yet, somehow, I had managed to hold it together. The desert had toughened me, but I knew that it was the hard granite and high-altitude passes of the Sierra Nevada that would prove me capable or not. I'd come out the other side destroyed, or steel.

CHAPTER 14
KENNEDY MEADOWS, CALIFORNIA

DAY 17 (CONTINUED) / 35 MILES

I devoured a salmon burger and fries with one hand while sorting through my resupply box with the other. Dozens of other thru-hikers were milling around and I felt a bit overwhelmed. Since I'd started nearly three weeks before I had yet to see this many hikers in one place. *I survived the desert.* It was my only thought and I felt immense accomplishment and relief. Somehow, I'd made it farther than I had thought possible and I tried to focus only on that, not what was to come. I polished off my celebratory burger.

I talked briefly to a few people, but most were busy in their own cliques—camaraderie forged by crossing seven hundred miles of desert together. However, one woman walked over to my table and struck up a conversation.

"Are you thru-hiking?" she asked.

"Yes. Are you?"

"Yes. With my husband. Are you solo?"

"Yeah."

"That takes guts." She sat down beside me. "I couldn't help but notice you hike in a skirt. Is it comfortable?"

"Oh, yeah. It's really cool and comfy. Lighter than pants. Not to mention it makes it easier to pee," I added.

She laughed. Her blond hair was clean and shiny in the sunlight. I realized that I wanted to take a shower.

"This is my new dress," I said, pulling a polka-dotted sundress out of the box and handing it to her. "The skirt I wore across the desert is shredded."

"Oh, that is light!" She handed it back to me.

"Could I ask you a favor?" I felt shy asking a stranger for help. "Would you be willing to watch my things while I dash over and take a quick shower?"

"Of course!"

"I'll be right back." I took my new dress and hurried over to the outside shower stall. It was only my third bathing of the entire hike.

A few tears of gratitude ran down the drain with the bubbles and dirt. They were not shed for just soap and water, but also for a brief friendship at a picnic table in the midst of a 2,600-mile-long trek. They were because I knew I had sacrificed having a trail family, fellowship, and community in order to achieve the audacious goal I'd chosen.

I returned to the table, clean and in a new dress that I'd mailed myself. Although the skirt had been shredded by the desert flora, I still had the long-sleeved white blouse my mother had sewn for me to wear across the desert in 2005—and it was still in good condition.

"Thank you!" I said to the woman sitting by my things. She said goodbye and disappeared into the store.

I picked up the shirt and sniffed it. It had now taken me from Mexico to Kennedy Meadows twice, enfolding me in my mother's love across every dry mile. It was filthy and it stank. Nonetheless, I couldn't just throw it away. I folded it carefully and set it in my now empty resupply box alongside my desert umbrella. I shut the box with tape borrowed from the store and arranged for the owner to mail it home. *Perhaps that shirt will make this journey with me yet again.*

CHAPTER 15
SOUTH SIERRA WILDERNESS, CALIFORNIA

DAY 17 (CONTINUED) / 35 MILES

As I set out down the road, I enjoyed the rejuvenated feeling brought on by a clean body, new dress, and full belly. Unfortunately, I was also keenly aware of the dramatically increased pack weight—six days of food and nearly a gallon of water. While my pack wasn't as heavy as when I'd walked north from Kennedy Meadows in 2005—forty-one pounds— it had soared from ten pounds to thirty pounds over the course of a morning. Adding to the discomfort was the hard-plastic bear canister, required by Sequoia and Kings Canyon National Parks, pushing into my back and tailbone. Because of the many bears habituated to humans and their food, everyone camping in the backcountry was required to store their food in a bear canister one hundred feet from their tent while they slept. Thru-hikers were no exception and every one hated the bulk of the canister and how poorly they fit into ultra-light backpacks. I'd tried several ways to put mine in my pack before I'd left. There was only one, and it hurt. The last time I'd left Kennedy Meadows I had literally cried from the weight of my pack during the initial climb to the bluffs above the South Fork of the Kern River. This time, I set my jaw against the discomfort and hiked up the winding trail.

On my whole itinerary, there were only two times that I would have to carry six days of food between resupply points. Ironically, they coincided with the burliest portions of the trail. This was the first. As dusk fell, I gave in to the fatigue and aching of my body. The heavy pack had worn me out completely, even though I wanted to go farther. I plopped my pack into the dirt beside a spreading pine tree. Free of my untoward load, I lurched around staking my tent out as taut as I could against the gusting winds.

DAY 18 / 44 MILES

The climb up to the Olancha Pass junction was prolonged, although not particularly steep. I waded through false hellebore and other wildflowers, trying desperately not to think about how much my shoulders ached. Over and over I told myself that the next week—crossing the High Sierra—was likely to be the crux of the entire journey. I just had to maintain a forty-mile-per-day average over the high passes and not break.

"If you can reach the mellower terrain of Northern California you might be able to set this record, Anish." I gave myself pep talks aloud to drown out the doubts.

The trail entered Death Canyon and I was struck by the beauty of where I was. The name did nothing to capture the sun-dappled pine forest and cool breezes. My fatigue melted. There was no other place I would rather be. I climbed steadily upward, gazing down at the bright green meadows below me. An hour later I heard the music that every desert traveler longs to hear. I rounded a slight bend and saw clear, cold water streaming across the trail. Parting the upslope bushes, I saw Poison Meadow Spring gushing from the rocks. It looked nothing like its name implied. I chugged as much pure spring water as I could hold. The sun was past its peak as I set out, refreshed. The sloshing of clean water in my pack made me so happy that I didn't even mind the added weight. A few miles ahead of me lay 11,145-foot Cottonwood Pass, which, in my mind, was the true end of the desert and the beginning of the High Sierra.

In 2005, an unusually heavy snow year, I had approached this pass without knowing how long it would take us to plow through the snow-blanketed mountains ahead. Before leaving Kennedy Meadows, I had left a message for my mom that if she didn't hear from me within two weeks, something had happened to us and she should call for help.

This year was far more normal, perhaps even a bit on the dry side. It worked in my favor. I would be able to make good time through the first serious mountain range, unhindered by lots of lingering snow. Knowing this, I hadn't mailed myself an ice axe or traction for my shoes. Omitting the extra weight from my pack would also help me move faster. I anticipated a predominantly wide-open trail with only a few snowy patches on the north-facing slopes of passes.

Golden light illuminated the meadows below Cottonwood Pass. I hiked upward into the cooling air, relishing the beauty. As I reached the pass, I found a group of men getting ready to descend the trail that led away from the crest. We chatted briefly and they mentioned patchy snow and plentiful water ahead. I thanked them and continued as the sun began to set.

A mysterious phenomenon occurs at night on the trail. You start to slow down, even though your perception is that the pace is the same. I obsessively checked my app to confirm that the vague trail through sandy soil and standing stones was, in fact, still the PCT. Each time I dipped to cross a stream, I looked around hopefully for Rock Creek Campground. Near 11 p.m. I finally found it. A dozen tents dotted the forest and meadow, so I searched the perimeter for a vacant spot. The only protected one I could find was a tiny space inside a triangle of trees. I nestled my tent into it and, even though it touched branches and the trunks, I was sheltered from the rising wind. I hoped the canopy of leaves would also counteract the condensation caused by camping near a river.

CHAPTER 16
SEQUOIA AND KINGS CANYON NATIONAL PARKS, CALIFORNIA

DAY 19 / 40 MILES

My watch alarm woke me to dull, gray light. No more golden desert sunrises. Rather than starting the day in dry heat, everything was damp from nearby Rock Creek. I packed rapidly in the unfamiliar cold. For the first time on the hike I wore my thin fleece gloves and beanie. Stiff, stumbly, and foggy-brained, I tried to hike fast to warm up without much success. Near the crossing of Rock Creek, I passed another thru-hiker packing up his cowboy camp—he'd slept under the stars with no tent. I quietly wished him a good morning, which he returned.

After splashing through icy Rock Creek, I began to switchback upward. The weight of the bear can and five days of food was unpleasant, but I was thankful that the effort was warming my bones. I came to a small trickle and paused to get water. My jacket was on top of my water bladder so I yanked it out of my pack and dropped it onto a rock.

"Clink!"

With a sinking feeling, I picked it up and felt the pocket. Sure enough, my SteriPEN was inside the jacket pocket where I had left it the night before. I clicked it on and put it into my bottle. No lights.

"Dammit."

I shook it and tried again. Nothing. I swapped out the batteries. Still nothing. I ripped open my Aqua tabs and threw one in. I shoved my jacket and broken SteriPEN back into my pack and shouldered it just in time to see the man I'd passed at Rock Creek coming up the trail. We climbed in silent unison a switchback apart. He slowly gained on me until we crested the ridge together and, in unspoken agreement, headed for a sun-drenched log nearby.

"Climbing Whitney?" he asked as I took off my jacket, gloves, and hat.

"No, not this time." I crammed an entire granola bar into my mouth, not caring how rude it was.

"You've hiked the PCT before?" He pulled some trail mix out of his nearly empty food bag.

I nodded and picked my pack up.

"Well, enjoy your hike."

I struggled to swallow most of the food in my mouth. "You too!"

I turned and headed down toward Crabtree Meadow and the John Muir Trail junction.

Now in the sun, the verdant meadows seemed welcoming rather than clammy. Mounts Chamberlin, Newcomb, Hitchcock, and Whitney—the highest mountain in the Lower 48—towered above me as I strode northward. The gray granite was austere, softened by the water, snow, and vegetation that had been lacking over the previous seven hundred fifty miles. I crossed Crabtree Creek and merged with the John Muir Trail. From here, the Pacific Crest Trail would run concurrent with this much older trail for over one hundred miles through the valleys and passes of the High Sierra. I rolled through the unique landscape south of Forester Pass, marveling at the bleached white rocks and sparse pine trees dotting the terrain. *There is more water here than in all of Southern California's PCT combined.* As I reached an open, rocky basin, I slid back into my shell jacket. The intense solar radiation at over eleven thousand feet seared my skin despite the sunscreen I'd slathered on. Ahead of me lay a seemingly impenetrable wall of rock. However, because I'd been there before, it was easy to pinpoint the tiny notch where the trail went through Forester Pass. It seemed impossible that the Pacific Crest Trail could take you there, yet I knew that it did. I picked my way through melt pools and rocks, searching for trail, as I crossed occasional snow patches. The path curved due east and then began to switchback up through solid rock.

My watch beeped and I reached into my pack for something to eat. My hand encountered a large, squishy bag. I pulled out the gallon ziplock that contained a pound of peanut butter and twenty ounces of grape jelly and bit one corner off. I squeezed some of the contents into my mouth like piping frosting. *This is like eating the world's biggest gel pack.*

As I climbed, I marveled at the engineering difficulties this route must have presented as the CCC blasted the John Muir Trail into place decades ago. The narrow path was literally etched from the side of the cliff by dynamite. I pushed myself upward even though gravity fought to pull my pack backward. Altitude made my heart race and my head ache, but I knew that pushing through minor altitude sickness was what it would take. I had to not only reach the top of this pass, but also drop 2,500 feet and ascend 1,200 more in order to cross Glen Pass—which was still twelve miles away—by nightfall.

I dropped into a heap beside the sign marking the top of the pass at 13,153 feet—the highest elevation of the entire PCT. I sucked wind for a few seconds, happy to see that there was a well-beaten path through what little snow remained on the north side. After eating a snack, I set out toward the valley below—laughing, plunging, and sliding through slushy snow. Climbing was difficult with the lack of oxygen and increased pack weight, but playing in the snow and slip-sliding down from the pass was not. In the transition zone from snow to bare earth, the trail meandered past jewel-blue pools formed from the melt. No doubt they'd all vanish as summer wore on.

The miles along Bubbs Creek before the turnoff for Glen Pass elapsed effortlessly. I turned right and trudged upward, dreading the long climb. Along the way, I paused briefly to gaze down at Charlotte Lake. Late afternoon light sparkled across its surface, and all around me the pine trees glowed. I drank in the glorious, gold-lit basin, basking in the beauty that had entranced John Muir himself.

I reeled my mind back in from the vista when the trail rounded a bend and I tripped on uneven rocks. I fell, banging my knee. Cursing aloud at the impact, I wished for the hundredth time I had trekking poles. I couldn't believe that I'd hiked the entire Triple Crown without them and hardly ever taken a tumble. I seemed to trip constantly this time on the PCT. Chalking it up to fatigue, I assessed the blood streaking down my leg. I sucked some water from my hose and spit it onto the scrape and smeared some antibiotic ointment on the gash. My reverie was over. It was back to business.

I must get to the pass before dark. I must get to the pass before dark. Over and over the one thought raced through my brain. Sucking down a caffeinated gel, I put my hands on my hips and pushed upward. I looked down at my feet. *One in front of the other, climb, climb, climb.*

Shadows lengthened and overcame the basin as I wound my way past tarns and giant boulders. My legs turned to jelly as the oxygen available to them dwindled. My anemia was making altitude harder on me. I reached a set of long, sweeping switchbacks that carried me above a deep, indigo lake. I had always felt a strong sense of foreboding near Glen Pass—it was a thin place, an intersection of the spiritual and physical realms where I did not want to linger. I looked up at the jagged ridge above me. It looked impossible to cross . . . and so far away.

I leaned against the rock wall, letting it momentarily take the weight of my pack off of my shoulders. The veins in my temples throbbed as I stared up at the lavender sky. *I'm so dizzy.* My heart pounded against my ribs as though it was trying to escape. I placed my hands on my waist and leaned forward to begin hiking again. Beneath my fingertips I felt my pulse, strong and fast, coursing through my abdomen. I leaned back against the rock.

"Maybe I should just wait here a few more minutes," I told myself.

Deep inhalation . . . 2 . . . 3. Slow exhalation . . . 2 . . . 3. Deep inhalation . . . 2 . . . 3. Over and over I counted, focusing on bringing as much oxygen into my body as I could. I left my hand resting lightly on my belly. After a few minutes I could no longer feel my heartbeat palpably beneath it. After a few more breaths, the intense throbbing in my head subsided. Only then did I dare to lean forward—accepting my full pack weight—and began climbing again.

I reached the top of Glen Pass at 11,926 feet just as the sun kissed the horizon. In all directions the silhouettes of jagged peaks stood starkly against the darkening sky. It was hard to believe that a well-trodden path would take me through them. I had about an hour of light remaining as I looked down and surveyed the intermittent snow below me. My eyes traced the route as it dropped two miles and 1,500 feet down to Rae Lakes, reaffirming my memory. From there it would be another six miles downstream along the river to where I would camp. Shivering, I slipped into my jacket and headed down the snowy, shadowed side of the pass.

I crossed between the lakes just before dark. As I neared the ranger station I found ice cold water gushing from a vegetated slope. Confident it was a spring, I filled my bladder and drank my fill without a chlorine tablet. I pulled out a snack and crammed it into my mouth, chewing while I fitted my headlamp onto my head. It was still a long descent to Woods Creek. I clicked on my light and began to walk.

I passed tents nestled into beautiful campsites alongside gushing streams. I wished I, too, was inside my tent, lazily reflecting on the day and preparing to sleep for nine hours. As I walked into the darkness, I reflected on my choice. I'd chosen this challenge for many reasons, and one of the greatest was to face the darkness, both without and within. Daily my body preferred to quit hours before I did. Instead I continued on, because of my stubbornness, yes, but also to allow scars to form when I wrestled with grief, memories, loss, and destiny on a sliver of trail in the moonlight. I was opening myself to true healing by finally dealing with my wounds. Sometimes all I had to do was acknowledge my own stubbornness. Others I had to rip off old scabs and let new ones form into thicker, beautiful scars.

I'd failed to live up to the expectations of my parents. I had not utilized my education in any real way and I'd given up on marriage. For the first time, I accepted that I could not meet the expectations of others and make myself happy at the same time. Being true to myself had led me here—onto a wild trail in the middle of the night—not into a nine-to-five and the creation of my own family. I hated myself for not being able to conform happily. I hated myself for trying and failing. I loved myself for choosing to do what was right for me, no matter the cost. I forgave myself for trying to please others when I knew it wasn't right for me.

Now, nearly three weeks of nights into the challenge, I began to find comfort in the dark hours, even though they were difficult. I'd realized that everyone was beautifully scarred by life's wounds. Before, I hadn't thought of my scars as beautiful, but in facing my fears, and myself, in the dark hours I saw that scars denote healing—they tell our story of triumph. They proclaim our ability to overcome, and to face the Night.

I reached a small creek and crossed on a convenient log, but there was no sign of the trail on the other side. Climbing up a steep slope, I wandered around before referencing the Halfmile app. It confirmed that I was on the trail. But I wasn't. I wandered some more, finally stumbling down a slope where I found the trail. I had crossed prematurely and, in the darkness, missed the true crossing twenty feet away. Wandering within the app's error margin for ten minutes without seeing the trail reminded me again of the inadequacy of my ancient headlamp. I wished I'd had enough money to buy a newer, brighter one before I'd started my hike.

Fueled by frustration and wasted energy, I stormed down the trail as it paralleled Woods Creek. Time seemed indeterminate as I moved through the dark, with no landmarks to gauge my progress. Finally, my light reflected off the guy lines of a tent. Hopeful that I was near the campsite, my pace increased. Another tent came into view . . . and another. Soon, I was at the huge suspension bridge across Woods Creek. Aiming my light downward so as to not wake anyone, I quickly found a flat area away from the other tents. I set up and crawled inside, wriggling into my wool base layers before lying down.

I gazed out of the mesh of my tent into the ink black silence. The next day had loomed in my mind since I first wrote it on the map. It was a huge, seemingly impossible challenge—one that would break me or prove me worthy to continue. From this campsite I would need to travel up and over three high passes: Pinchot, Mather, and Muir. There would be nearly ten thousand feet of climbing (and an almost equal amount of descent) over the forty miles. The thought was too overwhelming to dwell on.

DAY 20 / 40 MILES

I crossed the bridge over roaring Woods Creek in the morning twilight. There was something about seeing the first desperately awaited ray of dawn color the horizon ahead of me. It awakened a thankfulness, not only for the strength of my body, but for my life itself. I realized that no matter how dark, no matter how long or cold or alone, I would hold the promise of dawn in my heart. *No matter the outcome, I will be thankful for the strength of my body—for the blessing of being alive. For the opportunity to face the night.* I wound through beautiful meadowlands as I climbed toward Pinchot Pass, drinking in the wildflowers drenched in dew and sunrise.

I reached the pass at 8 a.m. and scarfed a second breakfast before descending into the basin. There, I enjoyed passing multiple campsites full of people rising for the day. The chronic stiffness in my body had subsided over the last forty-eight hours, and I didn't even notice the continual aching in my feet anymore. At the same time, my mood had elevated to the heights of the passes I crossed. I continued to follow the trail through its cycles of pass-valley-pass—descending from the ridge-line to ford a deep river in the valley below and climbing again to the next ridgeline. I reached the fourth of the five highest passes on the PCT—Mather Pass—at midday and sat down for a quick snack.

"I actually feel pretty damn good," I stated to a bird perched nearby, waiting for a handout.

Just then a hiker popped over the north side of the pass. He sat beside me and struck up a conversation.

"Are you a PCT thru-hiker?"

I nodded, my mouth full of prunes.

"Are you trying to break the record?"

I stared at him for a long while before I answered. It was obvious that he already knew who I was and what I was trying to do. The hair on my neck prickled.

"Yes," I replied cautiously.

"I thought I might run into you. I do a loop out here every year. Although I usually go the other way, I wanted to meet the Ghost. So I went the opposite direction this time."

"What is with the name the Ghost? My name is Anish." I was irritated despite my nervousness at obviously being stalked.

He looked at me quizzically for a moment.

"It's what people are calling you on the PCT-Listserv. You're here one minute, gone the next. All anyone sees are your unusual footprints."

I looked down. He was right, the Altra shoes I wore left lug patterns in the shape of a bare foot in the dirt. I'd heard of the PCT-Listserv, or PCT-L for short. I'd never been on it because like all online forums it seemed to be full of haters and belligerent trolls. Drama had never been my scene and I certainly didn't want it to ever be a part of my trail experience.

He asked a few more probing questions, seeming intrigued, but cautious.

"But how do they know about me?" I asked, incredulous that some random strangers on the internet should know what I was doing, much less christen me with a new trail name. "From my Facebook page?"

"No. Just the forums. Some people you met along the way have posted there. Now there's a whole thread where people post sightings of you or your footprints. Or where you've signed in at registers."

It was decidedly creepy. I stood up and shouldered my pack.

"Many people find the idea of a woman going after Scott Williamson's record to be . . . interesting." He spoke slowly, pausing as if searching for the right word to describe what people felt.

I inferred from his articulation that I wasn't being taken seriously. It bothered me even though I myself had doubts. Of course people were dubious—I had no trail cred in the realm of FKTs. I had no sponsors. I carried a worn-out sleeping bag and a dim headlamp with corroded battery ports. I wore a dress I'd gotten for a dime at a thrift store. But it was his tone in saying *woman* in that final sentence that sent me into an internal rage. *Misogynistic assholes!* Nothing galvanized my resolve more than being told I couldn't do something—especially because I am a woman.

"It's been nice talking to you. I hope the rest of your hike is great. But I have to get going now. I have twenty miles and another pass to cross today."

I wondered what he felt now that he had seen "the Ghost" in the flesh. I turned my gaze toward the Palisade Basin. This woman was going over Muir Pass tonight.

"Good luck," he said.

With that, I started descending.

In and of itself, the twenty miles from where I stood to Muir Pass was an incredibly long day. Heading there at 1 p.m.—after already climbing two passes—seemed insane. Even though I could finally move without aches, pains, and stiffness I was still dogged by constant weariness. In fact, when I had first arrived at the top of Mather I was so spent I wanted to take a nap. Until I'd gotten angry. *Three of the highest Sierra passes in one day? Impossible. What was I thinking when I made my schedule?* I plunged into the soft snow on the switchbacks—plowing forward and down—toward the upper lake in the basin. *Insane or not this is what I'm here to do.*

The descent to the shimmering Palisade Lakes was quick and soon I was flying down the so-called "Golden Staircase" of tightly packed switchbacks hewn into the granite. The staircase deposited me into the thick pine forest of the valley and I turned upstream alongside the Middle Fork Kings River. I began the gentle ascent of LeConte Canyon—up through woods crisscrossed with rivers—settling into a steady pace that I could maintain on the extended climb back to 11,955 feet. My weariness was juxtaposed with an intense craving to reach my intended camp for the night.

As I pressed deep into the High Sierra, I was surprised by my ability to climb and descend so quickly while lugging a heavy pack. Here, on the cusp of crossing the last of the highest passes, I felt invigorated.

I felt as though I were about to fight something bigger than myself, even though I knew that within me was where the true battle resided.

It was almost dusk and people were bedding down early—staging themselves for the ascent of Muir Pass in the morning. I wished I could do the same. I waved at a camp of thru-hikers clustered around their tiny stoves and one man called out, "Are you heading for the pass tonight?"

"Yep!"

"Yeah! Go get it!"

His enthusiasm put a little extra pep in my step and I pushed onward. Deep shadows poured over the summits, drowning the lakes below them. Venus shone bright, but brief. Soon I was walking by headlamp alone. The dirt path became rockier and harder to discern, especially with meltwater flowing across everything. Before long there were patches of snow to contend with as well. My pace became a repetition of hike, stop, search, find, and continue. I frequently wondered if my wandering was even making progress.

My forehead ached from squinting as I searched for cairns and footprints. I forded and reforded dark, cold water unnecessarily, uncertain whether I was ankle-deep in meltwater or rivers unless fish brushed against my bare legs. Night air atop the passes and peaks cooled rapidly and rushed downslope—I shivered as these katabatic winds washed over me. My pace became a crawl and I cried in frustration after following cairns far off the trail and onto a jut of land above Helen Lake. I was at a dead-end viewpoint. The trail was on the other side. I scrambled down the rocks and forded the thigh-deep outlet. The fear of falling into the black, cold water gripped my stomach and knotted it. I just wanted to be away from this landscape of snow, water, and rock. Pulling out my phone, I turned on the Halfmile app—walking while staring at the screen to ensure I didn't veer too far from the trail again.

Finally, I felt a slight shift in the nature of the route. I started climbing up and away from the dark and menacing pools of water. As the trail switchbacked, relief began trickling into my mind. The air grew warmer as I climbed steadily under the stars. I rounded another switchback and felt—rather than saw—the pass before me. I knew it was close. A frog serenade greeted me and waves of homesickness washed over me. Tears welled in my eyes as I thought of laying in my bed only a few weeks before, laughing at how the riotous cacophony of frogs in the creek just outside my window made it hard to fall asleep. It seemed like another lifetime. *It was another lifetime.*

A few strides later the outline of a beehive-shaped emergency shelter—Muir Hut, the top of the pass—came into view. When I reached it, I clicked off my light. The night sky illuminated silhouettes of grandeur in all directions, their jagged peaks serrating the edges of the starry blanket above. *It's 11 p.m. I did it. All three passes.* Tears rolled down my face with only God and the stars to see. *I covered all five of the high-altitude passes in two days.* For the first time since I'd left Campo I realized something more than the depth of my exhaustion. I realized the depth of my thankfulness, and of my joy.

DAY 21 / 39 MILES

After the huge passes of the High Sierra, the altitude drop to eight thousand feet and the level elevation profile made the miles fly by effortlessly. Contentment from doing what I had set out to do overrode all fatigue. I hiked with a giant smile plastered across my face. As I descended the dusty trail toward the tiny resort and trail riding outpost of Reds Meadow, I tried not to think about the cold beverages and greasy food a stone's throw from the PCT. *It's not a scheduled stop.* I reminded myself sternly that I would be in Tuolumne Meadows where there was a camp store, restaurant, and my resupply box the next day. At the junction my feet turned toward Reds Meadow.

In the store, I bought a cold soda, a few candy bars, and sundries. I also rummaged through the hiker box, nabbing a few odds and ends that looked good. Back outside, I sat on a stump near a cluster of other thru-hikers drying their tents, eating greasy food from the grill and talking boisterously. I pawed through my pack in search of every last bit of garbage. When I reached the broken SteriPEN, I threw it with extra force into the nearest trash can, still angry at having carried it for so long. Then I used duct tape from the hiker box to tape the sponge I had just bought to my backpack's right shoulder strap. Deep welts had formed on my clavicle where the strap dug into my flesh. It hurt every second of every day and I was desperate to alleviate the pain.

While I tried to be efficient with the unplanned town stop, I half listened to the banter of the other hikers. They had yet to take notice of me, and my seclusion made it seem as if all seven of them were talking at top volume simultaneously.

"Yeah, she's doing like forty miles EVERY DAY!"

"I don't know how anyone can do that."

"I don't think anyone can do that."

"Do you think she can actually beat Scott's record?"

I smiled a little. If I couldn't block their voices out, at least I could be amused by their conversation. I finished trash patrol and pack repair, and shifted to spooning hiker box tuna into my mouth. One of the hikers nearest me seemed to notice my presence for the first time. He pointed at the sponge and duct tape padding.

"What's that for?"

"Pack is rubbing my shoulder." I pointed to a raw area the size of a silver dollar. "I'm just trying to add padding to the strap to keep it from getting worse."

"God, that looks like it hurts!"

I nodded. The nearby conversation circulated back to the woman hiking the trail at a blistering pace, trying to set a record. He turned to interject a thought and then looked back at me.

"What do you think? Have you heard about her? Do you think she can do it?"

"Well, yeah, I certainly hope she can do it since I'm her."

He stared at me, taking in my dirty body and MacGyver'd pack. "WHAT?! Hey! Guys! This is HER!"

There was absolute silence for about three seconds. Then came a cavalcade of questions interspersed with encouraging words. I struggled to interject answers. Everyone was talking at once.

"When did you start?"

"June 8."

"How far did you walk already today?"

"Thirty miles."

"Incredible!"

"How many passes did you do every day?"

"Two or three."

"How much does your pack weigh?"

"I think about twenty pounds usually."

"Three passes in one day?! Amazing."

I left shortly thereafter feeling like I had made new friends, even if I'd never see them again. When I reached the PCT, I saw a group of hikers next to the trail drinking beer and relaxing. They hailed me and I said hello back. I had lost a significant amount of time stopping during the day, but the positive mental state I'd gained from human interaction was worth it.

Unfortunately, it didn't last.

The mosquitoes swarmed without warning—biting and whining. The beasts whirled around me, attacking every centimeter of bare skin. I flailed desperately while I hiked as fast as I could, desperate to get away. I could fully understand why a moose would run off of a cliff to escape them. Being surrounded by thousands of tiny predators could send even a rational human into a blind panic.

Finally, the trail climbed high onto a ridge where there was a light breeze. For the first time in several hours I finally felt like I could relax. My mosquito-panic eased, though I still hiked quickly to make up for lost time. I wasn't sure how much camping there would actually be on the rocky ridgeline, but I hoped I'd find something. Otherwise, I would have to descend to Thousand Island Lake and the guaranteed thicket of mosquitoes blanketing it.

An hour later I found a wide spot just below the trail—a cliffy overlook rather than the soft ground I was looking for. I decided that it was a great place to call home for the night. Despite lying on a slab of granite, I found it surprisingly easy to relinquish consciousness.

CHAPTER 17

YOSEMITE NATIONAL PARK, CALIFORNIA

DAY 22 / 38 MILES

Inside my tent, I sat massaging my filthy, chafed feet. Examination by headlamp revealed that the blister on my left heel was nearly healed. I peeled back the tape on my right heel. That blister was far from repaired. I carefully removed the tape so as not to rip off any tender skin, rubbed hand sanitizer on it, and applied triple antibiotic ointment. Then I slid my wool sleep socks on. Either the wound would heal or it wouldn't—I wasn't going to be able to baby it forever. I decided that in the morning I would tape over it and forget it. Hopefully it wouldn't become infected, but I'd done all that I could do at this point. Keeping it clean would be a losing battle that I didn't want to spend time fighting any more.

I laid back and stared at the moonlit silhouettes of trees through my nearly transparent cuben fiber tent. Steps away from where I lay, someone had spelled out "1000" across the trail with small stones. Tears oozed out of the corners of my eyes and rolled toward my ears and down my neck, soaking into the wool shirt I slept in. I'd covered 41.6 miles per day for twenty-two days. Unfathomable. Yet, more unfathomable was that despite the hardship and the incredible effort of hiking one thousand miles, I was not even halfway through the attempt.

"Will this ever become easier?" I whispered to the trees.

Time had ceased to exist in a meaningful way, except when I thought about how much longer I had to go. On the one hand, I felt as though I had only been out for a week, but, on the other, accumulated sleep deprivation and the physical stress of hiking day in, day out also made it feel like six months.

"How can I possibly do this for thirty-six more days?" I asked. The trees swayed in silence.

CHAPTER 18

MOKELUMNE WILDERNESS, CALIFORNIA

MICHIGAN / AUGUST 1990

"Storms coming. Want to go?"

My dad had just clicked off the radio and was lacing up his brown leather work boots. I slipped my feet into a pair of flip-flops and followed him to the truck. I was nine years old and there was no way I was going to miss a chance to chase storms with him. He threw the truck into drive and spun gravel as we veered onto the dirt road.

"Where are we going?"

"Palo."

To the west, the sky was the color of a healing bruise—deep blue with pale green edges. Lightning flickered repeatedly and I could hear thunder, even over the sound of the engine. Clouds to the northwest swirled ominously. I told myself that in the Navy my dad had dropped instruments from the belly of cargo planes right into the heart of Guamanian typhoons—all in the name of science. He knew what he was doing. I wiggled my toes and tried to keep my face neutral.

My dad glanced over at me.

"You scared?"

"No."

"OK."

I was scared though. I was always afraid on these high-speed drives into the booming, flashing, hailing maw of a storm.

"Shit."

The truck jolted as he slammed on the brakes and swung onto yet another dirt road. We were speeding due north now—right toward the black wall of the tempest ahead of us. Rain came fast and thick as though we'd driven into an automated car wash. I couldn't see the hood of the truck even with the wipers on at max speed. He came to a halt in the middle of the road.

Thunder shook the vehicle as blinding flashes of lightning came simultaneously from all directions. I tightened my grip on the seat cushion and wiggled my toes faster. Suddenly I heard the roar of a train.

"Hold on."

Something slammed into the truck. I couldn't hold back. I started to cry.

"Heather. It's OK. It's OK. It's just wind."

The rain began to subside, its deafening roar petering out into a gentler sound. My dad put the truck back into gear. I stared out the window, taking in all my surroundings again now that I could see. A nearby cornfield was flattened.

"Do you want to go home?"

"No," I bawled, trying to be brave.

"OK." He turned east.

Twenty minutes later we pulled into our driveway. A rainbow arced across the sky, the foreboding clouds nothing but a memory.

"Don't tell your mom about this, OK?"

Nodding, I got out of the truck. I ran into the house, past my mom, and into my room. Crawling into bed, I clung to my teddy bear and cried all the fear out. Downstairs I could hear their voices.

"Andy, she's only nine years old!"

"I didn't know there'd be a microburst near us."

"She can't go again. Ever."

A storm was brewing. I could see it through the gaps in the trees, but I could also feel its ominous presence—as if I were being stalked by a volatile predator. At the next dirt road, I stopped at an embankment above a river to eat a snack and study the darkening sky.

I knew what the trail did next. It climbed up above the trees and canyon-like features to the exposed slopes of a mountain called The Nipple. From there it wound along the ridge—but for how long? That I couldn't quite remember. After about five minutes I stood up. The storm was getting closer. I had to either wait for it here or make a dash and hope that I could get across the exposed slopes before lightning danger became extreme. In the name of the record, I decided to be brave.

After a mile or two I stopped to get water from a trickling stream. I looked westward, awed by the hues of the discolored sky. Lightning cracked the dark countenances of the clouds again and again. I started second guessing myself. *Perhaps I should wait it out. No, I have to go. I can't afford to wait.* I pushed up the hill.

The mental weight of the bear canister still in my backpack dragged me down more than its physical weight did. It wasn't required after Yosemite National Park and I desperately wished that I could get rid of it, but I could not leave it alongside the trail and there'd been no trash cans at the Sonora Pass picnic area the day before. I calculated again . . . yes, I would reach Echo Lake tomorrow, a Sunday. There would be no way to mail it from there. I sighed and hauled on the pack straps that dug deeply into my shoulders. There was no choice then. I'd leave it at the Carson Pass Ranger Station near the trash cans.

A crack of thunder reverberated through my body. I thought my eardrums would explode from the percussion. I jerked my head up and looked around wildly. Storm clouds had completely filled the western sky. I turned around to see that another storm had arisen to the south. Now, the sky to the north was beginning to darken. I was being surrounded.

I could feel the panic of my nine-year-old self welling up from deep inside me. My feet moved faster on the scree—I was nearly to the summit of The Nipple. *I don't remember climbing so high.* Rain, propelled by wind, began to pelt me. Lightning and thunder came in a nearly steady stream. I thought of my father. He'd taught me to watch the clouds, to predict what they would do and read the messages they offered. I'd known this storm would build to humongous proportions, but I'd thought I would be faster. I hoped that wouldn't prove to be a fatal mistake of pride. *I'm sorry, Dad. I should've known better.*

The trail followed the ridgeline in front of me and I saw no evidence that it was going to descend anytime soon. I imagined pulling out my phone and calling my dad. Explaining my situation calmly even though I wanted to burst into tears. *What would he say?*

"Daddy, what should I do?" I yelled as if he could hear me, nearly three thousand miles away.

"Run like hell."

My dad's no-nonsense voice rang crystal clear. If I had not known better, I might have looked to see if I had actually dialed his number. Instead I yanked the hip belt straps so tight that they bruised me and I ran.

The movement was foreign. I couldn't lean properly and my legs couldn't piston fast enough. *I've forgotten how to run.* The pack bounced, slamming the bear can into my spine with every step. It rained harder and the sky around me sizzled. Hair prickled along my arms and neck, spurring me to run faster. My breath came in gasps as the impact of each step shot up my legs, jarring my body.

"Run like hell."

Those words came into my mind every time I started to slow down, urging me to pick up the pace. Lightning and thunder overlapped—simultaneously blinding and deafening. *The storms have converged on top of me.* I imagined myself running across Forbidden Mountain while Maleficent's rage whirled a storm into gargantuan proportions. In between gasps for air I prayed.

"Please God, protect me. I'll never be this stupid again."

After what seemed like an eternity, the trail dropped down into the forest. I slowed to my usual place, grateful for a respite from the jarring descent. The rain eased and then came down hard. As I continued onward through the trees, I could hear the beast growling overhead. I might be just out of reach of its fangs, but I was not truly safe. I climbed a bit and then dropped to a creek crossing. Mentally and physically exhausted, I sat down on the far bank to refill my water and eat something. I was a wreck—adrenaline still coursed through my veins, making me mildly nauseous. My back ached as though I had been beaten and I was shaking uncontrollably. Looking up, I could see that the sky to the east was dark with lightning crisscrossing it at intervals. Yet, the rain was falling lightly, and the bruised clouds above and behind me were breaking apart. The storm had passed.

I took a deep breath and headed upward.

Near the top of the broad pass sitting just below the peak called Elephants Back, I met a couple who was setting up their camp. Incredulous, I asked them if they'd been there during the storm. They said they'd been at the stream below and only started up when it seemed like the storm was going to break. We chatted and they seemed curious that I was going to continue on.

"I checked it out. The snow is pretty icy," the man warned.

"Thanks for the heads up. Enjoy your hike!"

I climbed the mellow pass, stepping carefully into the melted-out tracks near the top. They were indeed icy and I had to take my time. My fatigued legs shook from prolonged isometric contraction. As I left the snow behind and crested the ridge, I looked back and waved at the couple. They returned the salute. I headed downhill toward the ranger station and trailhead parking lot at Carson Pass.

In the parking lot I looked around for trash cans. There were none. The ranger station was locked up and no traffic was passing on the highway. I felt defeated. *Do I really have to carry these two pounds of empty plastic all the way to Echo Summit?* I couldn't bring myself to litter, even in a parking lot.

"The trash cans are in the privies."

I looked up to see a man with a thick beard and a couple of pairs of shoes sitting outside a camper. He was doing some sort of repair. I knew immediately that it was another thru-hiker.

"Thank you! Are you thru-hiking?"

"Yup. My wife and I. Her parents are crewing us from the camper for a stretch."

We exchanged small talk as I dug wrappers and trash from every nook and cranny of my pack and he attempted to repair his shoes with a tube of industrial glue. I piled my trash into the bear canister, walked to the privy, and dumped it into the garbage can. Walking back with the empty canister in my hands, I had an idea.

"Do you think your in-laws would be willing to mail my bear can home if I gave them some money? There's no rush. I won't need it again on the trip. Otherwise I'm just going to throw it away. I'm sick of carrying it."

"I can ask."

A few minutes later I was in the camper drinking juice and talking to an amazingly generous couple. I scribbled my address on a piece of paper and put it in the can with a twenty. They took it without question, even though it was an odd request. Trail magic!

I thanked them profusely and then started down the trail again. After nearly three hundred miles, my wounded spine was relieved to not have the hard plastic can banging against it. I watched the post-storm sky molt into a glorious sunset. Tomorrow I would walk past Lake Tahoe.

DAY 26 / 40 MILES

I crossed yet another ridge, passing a fallen ski boundary sign. Storms of emotion washed over me as I traversed shrubby, green slopes. One minute I was elated, the next I was sobbing. I missed life off the trail. I wanted to lay down and sleep my fill. The up and down feelings that came and went daily seemed to have no real triggers, though chronic sleep deprivation was likely the root cause. I yearned for sleep even more than for food. Yet, I was enraptured by the rolling beauty around me. Birdsong and babbling springs were the only music I desired. Every sunset and sunrise held a special beauty. I was stronger than I had known. I was also hungry, sunburned, and lonely.

After contouring below a ridgeline, I reached a trail junction. I glanced up toward the crest and then downward into the valley. *Was it only a year ago that I charged down that hill in a race, bound for the finish line on the track in Auburn? Reeling from a breakup and a winter when my health had bottomed out? It seems like a lifetime, or two, or three, ago now.* The race—Western States 100—was among the most prestigious trail ultramarathons in the United States. I'd had no business there, injured and undertrained. Much like the start of my PCT hike just a matter of weeks ago . . .

That one-hundred-mile ultramarathon had left me limping. I'd barely made the cutoff times and if it hadn't been for my pacer I probably wouldn't have. Yet what lesson had I learned from it? Certainly not the importance of training and being healthy before embarking on a huge endeavor. If that were the case I wouldn't be here now, thirteen months later, hobbling down the trail, intent on setting a Fastest Known Time.

Western States had been an exercise in overcoming adversity. As had the nine hundred miles I'd hiked on the PCT a few weeks afterward, where I'd wrestled the waves of emotion that threatened to swamp me the only way I knew how—by walking. Sorting through my feelings on the trail after leaving my job, moving out of my apartment, and losing a lover in quick succession had left me weak and strong at the same time. I learned how to put aside my emotions to get where I needed to go and, so far, that was the lesson that I had brought to this record attempt. It had proved vital in getting me to where I was now. Every day I let the irrational emotions spill out while I walked. I cried, yelled, pouted, swore . . . whatever I felt. But I never stopped walking.

The trail climbed gradually upward, breaking out onto the open, expansive crest. The rocky nubbin ahead was my namesake: Anderson Peak. I smiled, remembering the surprise I'd had after circling around and seeing it from a new angle the last time I was here: unassuming from the south, its north face dominated the view for miles.

I looked down at my battered shoes, filthy legs, and stained dress. My hip belt was cinched down almost as far as it could go. I felt small. It was an alien feeling. I'd never felt small before—except when Mother Nature raged, throwing lightning bolts and roaring thunder.

As the trail curved, the headwind I'd been pushing against suddenly shifted to a strong side wind. For a moment it was a relief. Then a gust slammed into my pack and spun me halfway around. With no chance to prepare myself, it flung me onto the rocky ground.

I pushed myself up and wiped the tears off my cheeks. Blood oozed from my kneecaps and scrapes on my hands and elbows. Above me, the cliffs of Anderson Peak's northerly face soared toward the sun. I braced myself for more wind gusts and marched onward, wincing. I knew that I wasn't much to look at but, just like Anderson Peak, my hidden side was indomitable.

CHAPTER 19
DONNER PASS, CALIFORNIA

DAY 27 / 40 MILES

Scott Williamson was a man of legend—the king of the PCT. He'd hiked the trail in its entirety more times than anyone else, including a northbound and southbound hike in the same season. Yet, for all those miles, he remained a mystery to most—many of the legends had been made up over the decades by hikers who'd never met him. I'd also never met him, although I'd seen a few pictures in an overly dramatic magazine portrayal years before. Still, I knew that his athleticism was unparalleled in the hiking world.

I thought about how, a few weeks before Campo, I had marked a fifty-kilometer ultramarathon course in the Chuckanut Mountains outside Bellingham. A local trail runner whom I'd never met had joined me to earn volunteer hours for a race entry requirement. In the course of conversation, I told him about my upcoming hike. He didn't know much about the Pacific Crest Trail or hiking culture, so I prattled on about the trail, the records Scott had set, and my own plans. He tried to draw comparisons to the ultrarunning world and its stars. I had adamantly protested that the physical ability necessary to set a self-supported FKT on a 2,600-mile-long trail was infinitely more impressive than running an ultramarathon, much less to have done it multiple times.

"Scott Williamson is by far the greatest athlete in the world," I finally said.

He was silent for a moment, tying a bit of flagging on a tree branch.

"So, you think you can break the record of the world's best athlete?"

It was an honest question. I stared at him, then the ground.

"Well, I guess I do."

He shrugged. Not much else was said on the topic. Yet his words flashed like neon lights in my mind as we marked the rest of the course. Over and over I wondered the same thing: *What on Earth was I thinking?*

After we parted ways at the parking lot, I organized a trunk full of race markings while processing the conversation. I still did truly believe that Scott was the greatest endurance athlete. But, what did that mean about me? I had barely finished Western States in twice the time it took other elite runners. For the first time, I realized with absolute certainty that I was doomed to fail. I'd had my suspicions before, but his words had taken reality and smacked me hard across the face. Unable to stop the plan I had set in motion, I was glad that I didn't know that runner . . . or Scott. My cheeks burned with embarrassment as I slammed the trunk shut and drove home. At least only one guy would know what a naive idiot I was—my hero need not ever know.

"Are you Heather?"

I snapped out of my reverie, startled by the voice. I had been walking on autopilot, only vaguely aware that a man was standing at the corner of a switchback.

I went from confused to guarded in an instant. The fact that this man knew my real name set off an alarm in my brain. All I could think of was the man on Mather Pass telling me about the discussions on the PCT-L. I studied him, looking for clues as to whether or not he was "safe." He wore a hat and sunglasses, which obscured his appearance, and was holding a brown paper grocery bag.

I nodded, still cautious. My gut instinct was that it was OK. We were only one switchback from the large parking lot off of the highway at Donner Pass. It was also the weekend. There were people everywhere. If I was wrong, I could scream and run. Someone would help.

"Hi, I'm Scott Williamson. I, uh, brought you some trail magic." He pulled off his sunglasses and held up the bag.

Flummoxed and starstruck, I walked with him up to the parking lot. We sat down at the edge and I devoured the wide variety of delicious food he'd brought me from the local organic food store.

"This is great salad! Thank you."

Meanwhile, only one thought ran through my mind: *Oh my God, I'm talking to Scott Williamson!*

As I walked away thirty minutes later, after shoveling in a ton of food in what was certainly an incredibly disgusting manner, I was dazed by the fact that I had just met my greatest athletic role model. I knew I'd had a conversation with him in between bites, but I couldn't remember a single word I'd said except "thank you." I turned back to ensure that the entire thing hadn't been a hallucination.

Scott waved and called with a smile, "Good luck! I hope you break my record . . . but not by too much."

"OK," I mumbled and hurried away. Once out of sight across the highway I sat down to compose myself. There was no way to avoid the embarrassment now: he knew. Overwhelmed by the irony, I laughed hysterically. But he'd also seemed impressed I'd made it this far and, despite the dry humor in his farewell, he had seemed sincere. *If he somehow thought I could . . .*

CHAPTER 20
SIERRA CITY, CALIFORNIA

DAY 29 / 37 MILES

Predawn light filled the forest and I clicked off my headlamp. A few minutes later I passed a tent. *No movement.* I smiled at the thought of the occupant still sound asleep. They would wake to find that a ghost had passed. When they arrived in Sierra City later today, probably racing darkness, I would already be fifteen miles past town, slipping my headlamp back on and preparing to walk into the night. I passed three other tents in short order as daylight began to pour through the pine boughs, staining the world gold.

It was early afternoon when I reached the highway and turned left. *One mile into town.* I'd already covered twenty miles, stopping only once for water. I was amazed at the way something had clicked in my body. The final hours of the day were still immensely difficult, and yet I found myself covering the first twenty to thirty miles without hardly thinking about it. *I'm a hiking machine.*

I reached the small town of Sierra City a short time later, and headed straight for the Red Moose Lodge, where I'd mailed my box. Dropping my pack on the picnic tables outside, I said a quick hello to the half dozen other hikers sitting there with their resupplies before walking into the dim building. I found one of the owners sitting behind the counter.

"Hi, my name is Heather Anderson. I sent a box here."

"Oh, yes, come on in to the storeroom. We've got so many boxes back here. Maybe you can recognize it?"

I followed the woman into the cluttered room behind the restaurant. She'd already informed me that the lodge was full and therefore no showers were available for hikers. I tried not to be disappointed, but I knew that there was a brand-new dress, socks, and shoes inside my box. I wanted nothing more than to be fully clean when I put them on.

"Oh yes, I am sure I can. It's covered with Care Bear stickers and purple duct tape." I had anticipated the piles of Priority Mail Flat Rate packages at my resupply points and had decorated my boxes to stand out.

She laughed at my description, but sure enough we spotted it immediately. It took some digging to unearth my box from the tower on top of it, but at last I carried it outside to the tables on the porch. Finding a place among the dozen or so other hikers lounging around, I kicked off my shoes and ripped open the box. I smiled as I pulled out a zebra-striped sundress I'd bought for a quarter at a thrift shop. It was ridiculous perhaps, but looking at it made me happy. The man sitting beside me looked at my piles with interest.

"Is there anything I can do to help you?"

"Uh, no, I don't think so."

"Are you sure? Anything? I really want to help you reach your goal."

"Nope, not unless you can find me a place to take a shower!" I joked. I hadn't told any of them what I was doing, but at this point I accepted that my mission was obviously preceding me, roaring up the trail grapevine like wildfire.

"OK!" He jumped up and took off down the street.

"Seriously?" I looked at the other hikers. They laughed.

I alternated eating chips with organizing the contents of my box into my pack. My internal clock was ticking. One hour was all I had budgeted for town and I'd already been there forty-five minutes. *How can time in town go so fast and time on trail go so slow?*

"Anish, I found you a shower."

I looked up to see the man standing on the sidewalk behind me, beaming.

"What?!"

"At the massage place down the road. Follow me."

I hopped over the low fence and followed him, clutching my new socks, shoes, and zebra dress.

"Now, the thing is they wanted $20."

"Oh, well thank you, but that's outside my budget," I interrupted him, stopping.

"I know. Which is why I went to the bar and there's a guy there who said he'd pay for it. The owner actually."

I stared at him incredulously for several seconds, then hurried after him. We stopped in front of the Old Sierra City Hotel. A bearded man sitting out front looked up at us.

"So, you're trying to set the record, huh?" he said.

"Yes."

"You ahead of Scott's time right now?"

"Well, yes, barely."

He roared, "I'll pay for your shower, but you gotta come back here and sign a dollar for my wall, OK?"

"Sure," I agreed. He pulled a worn leather wallet out of the pocket of his equally worn jeans and handed me a twenty.

"Thank you, so much! I'll, uh, be right back to sign the dollar."

My thru-hiker trail angel guided me across the street to My Sisters Cottage. There was a toddler running around the porch. The woman watching the child play looked at me with curiosity as I handed her the money. She pointed around the back. "Help yourself."

I turned to say something, but my angel was gone. I walked around the building and into the bathroom. Fancy shampoos and soaps, such as one would expect at a resort spa, sat on the shelves and in the shower. It was well decorated and there were fresh towels and candles. It was a jarring contrast to the dust, dirt, sweat, blood, and stench of the trail.

There was no one on the porch when I came back to the hotel bar. Pushing open the door, I found my angel inside holding a party cup. He raised it when he saw me. The bearded man waved me over to the counter.

"What can I get you? On the house. Beer?"

"Um, no, I still have to walk twenty miles today." I felt a slight panic. I'd certainly been here more than an hour now. *How long? Two hours? Three?*

"Sure?" The owner held up a cup and looked at me with a grin.

"How about a Coke?" He nodded and poured me one, sliding it across the counter with one hand while opening the cash drawer with the other. He pulled out a dollar and handed it to me with a black pen.

"Can I use that one?" I pointed to a pink marker in the jar by the register.

"Knock yourself out. Write whatever you want, just be sure to sign it. We put all the famous people on the wall."

I looked around to see that there were indeed signed dollars, photos, and posters plastering the place. I recognized some as actors and actresses.

I giggled as I scrawled "Anish was here" in pink and handed it back.

"All right!" He took it over to the wall and tacked it up. A few folks near us cheered.

My angel and I walked quickly back toward the Red Moose Lodge. I gulped down the cold Coke as we walked.

"Thank you. So much. I mean, I really appreciate it."

"No problem. I'm glad to help. I have a lot of good trail karma to pay forward after all that I've received on this trail already and we aren't even halfway."

"Can I ask you one more favor?"

"Sure!"

"Can you take a picture of me in front of the Sierra City PCT sign on the side of the lodge?"

"Absolutely!"

Three hours after I'd left the soft tread of the PCT, I was back on it. I'd had to turn down four different offers for a ride the mile back to the trail but the integrity of my pedestrian-only journey remained intact. And, I felt like a rock star. *In my zebra dress and pink sunglasses, I even looked like one! Well, maybe only a little.* I laughed at myself. Not too far ahead of me lay the halfway point, the first Cascade volcano, and . . . the Oregon border.

"Woohooooo!" I screamed.

CHAPTER 21
MIDDLE FORK FEATHER RIVER, CALIFORNIA

DAY 30 / 47 MILES

I felt strong as I crossed the Middle Fork Feather River. Gliding beyond mile forty-five, I cruised upstream and began the climb. The campsite I was destined for was at the top, so I mustered the strength to push past the nice campsites nestled on the banks of the river. I was on heightened alert as I hiked upward through the dark, silent forest. This was mountain lion country and every sound made me jump. At last, the climb subsided and the trail leveled off at an intersection of dirt roads—my predetermined stopping point. I scoured the available flat spots and found them littered with trash, toilet paper, and shit. Disheartened, I looked at the Halfmile app. The next viable place seemed to be at a creek crossing three miles ahead. It was already after 10 p.m. and I wasn't sure I had any more miles left in me for the day, but the thought of camping in sites full of fecal matter disgusted me enough that I decided to try.

The trail was fairly level as it sliced across a 45-degree slope. In vain, I scanned the pines and ferns above and below for a flat spot—there was nowhere to sleep. Even though I was already on edge, expecting an encounter, I was still startled when a mile or so later I saw glittering cat eyes ahead of me on the trail.

I stopped in my tracks, unable to get my tired mind to react rapidly. Barking weakly a couple of times, I halfheartedly waved my hands over my head. I was simply too exhausted to exert much energy scaring the mountain lion away. My fight-or-flight instinct was tapped.

The cat did not move or react to my lackadaisical efforts. I sighed deeply, realizing the depth of my fatigue. I didn't have the desire to confront this animal. I wished it would simply vanish. The cat, on the other hand, sat studying me, seemingly uninclined to relinquish the trail. I turned around and walked back about one hundred feet. Upslope, I spied a decent-sized tree. I clawed my way to it using my hands, toes, knees . . . everything I could dig into the steep hill of thick, loose duff. Behind the tree—just as I had expected—was a small spot where the tree had retained the slope. I scraped the duff aside to create a slightly more level surface and somehow managed to pitch my tent and crawl inside.

"Eat me if you want, but first I am getting some sleep, damn it," I mumbled as I faded away.

DAY 31 / 44 MILES

In the morning I was shocked to discover that I had managed to pitch a tent where I had—a tiny two-by-three foot space clinging to the base of the tree. It was truly a feat of engineering. I packed up and spread the duff back over the site so it looked undisturbed. Exhausted from so little sleep after hiking forty-seven miles, I headed out. My head ached and I felt sluggish as I climbed. But once I attained the ridgeline, bathed in early morning light, I was rejuvenated. The dazzle of the sun chased the cobwebs from my mind as well as the chill from my skin. At last I dropped to a highway crossing where I discovered a woman in a lawn chair with breakfast: fruit, coffee, and other staples.

"You must be Anish!" she proclaimed, waving me toward an empty chair.

"I am," I replied, dropping to sit on the ground next to another thru-hiker. "Is that coffee?!"

"And fresh blackberries, grapes, melon. Jumanji here has already eaten about a pound of fruit!"

We all laughed and I swigged the black coffee as quickly as I could without burning my mouth.

"Thank you so much! This is a wonderful surprise," I said, refilling my cup.

"You're welcome. I'm Nancy. I live down the road and I'm a trail angel for PCT hikers. Most of them come to my house, but I figured you wouldn't have time."

"It's very nice to meet you."

After drinking another cup of coffee, I set off with Jumanji. He and I hiked together and chatted as we wound our way along the pine needle–cushioned trail, through a forest full of chirping squirrels.

"So when did you start?" I asked.

"February 25. But I took a week off to go to a wedding before I went into the Sierras. How about you?"

"June 8."

"Damn. You're hiking what? Forty miles a day?"

"Yeah. That's the goal. I'm aiming to hike it in two months."

"Why?"

"The challenge I guess. To see if I can. I hiked the PCT eight years ago, but it just felt right to try and do it this way this time. Sort of a destiny I guess."

"I get that. I can't really say why I'm out here either, other than it just felt like the thing I needed to do."

Five miles later we popped out at another road crossing and there was Nancy again, along with some others. On her tailgate she had French toast, orange juice, more coffee, and some other delicious homemade goodies. It was heavenly, the opposite of dark nights facing lions alone. I ate and drank and basked in the light of angels, a hiking companion to talk to, and generosity.

Jumanji settled in to take a siesta under a bush a mile after the second road crossing. Nourished by food and empowered by caffeine, I maintained a fast and furious pace to the dry, exposed ridgeline far above the one-horse town of Belden. Waves of heat rose from stark, dry riverbeds as I descended. I had already lost a great deal of time that morning, so I planned to make Belden Town Resort—the only establishment in Belden—an efficient stop. *Just get water and throw away trash.* The trail passed right through the parking lot and I paused at a spigot on the porch to fill my water. The smell of the grill wafting out of the bar was irresistible. I went inside and downed glass after glass of ice water before devouring an order of fish and chips.

Outside again, I chastised myself. *Another hour lost.* Yet I knew that I needed the sustenance. My body was telling me with increasing insistence every day that it needed far more than I was giving it, and the climb out of Belden was a long one that I had dreaded since before I started the hike. It was a convoluted uphill full of meandering trail, descents, and uninteresting scenery. I remembered cursing it repeatedly in 2005. I decided to hike fast as the day cooled and get as far as I could in the darkness. *I've got to make up some of the wasted time.*

My feet were more tender than usual and the trail seemed rockier. Each step hit a blistered pressure point, sending jolts through my body. *Only two more miles . . .* As the night wore on, each step had me wincing and crying out like the wounded animal I was. My pace slowed as I navigated the rocks with tedious care. *Only one more mile . . .* The cracking of a branch to my left briefly pulled my attention away from my internal countdown to camp. I glanced over and caught a pair of eyes reflecting the wan beam of my low-lumen headlamp. They blinked and were gone. In my exhausted state I wasn't even sure if I'd seen them. Whatever was or wasn't there, either was or wasn't there—as long as it didn't get in my way on the trail I didn't care.

A few minutes later I heard a stick crack behind me. I continued limping up the trail, the hairs on the back of my neck prickling. Again a stick cracked, echoing through the woods just to my left. Finally, my basal instincts got a message through to my logical processor, piercing the fog of exhaustion in my brain.

"I am being followed." I uttered the words to make myself understand the gravity of the situation. *And I am doing one hell of a wounded animal impression.*

I grabbed a sturdy stick and used it to straighten and steady my body. I squared my shoulders and moved forward with confidence and strength I did not feel. Pain rocketed across my nerves with each step, but I refused to cry out. I maintained a measured pace. Every few minutes I heard the crack of a stick, but no closer than before. I was being followed, at a distance. *How long will I have to play this game?* I was almost to where I wanted to camp. I hoped the lion wouldn't force me farther.

I arrived at Myrtle Flat and began to scout for camping, keeping my guard up. I found a flat area away from the trail with a thick layer of pine needle duff covering it. It looked invitingly soft. Just as I decided to call it home for the night, something caught my eye. Nearby was a pile of sticks, leaves, and duff about two feet across and a foot high. It looked constructed. I stared at it, vaguely remembering what I had once read on an interpretive sign at a trailhead: *"Fiercely territorial, mountain lions mark their territory by making piles of debris at the corners."* I shouldered my pack again. No way in hell was I camping here, at the territorial boundary of an animal that had been stalking me.

Just then, the beam of a headlamp sliced through the darkness and a man's voice called out: "Hello?"

"Hello! Is there a place to camp by you?" I shouted. Before they could answer, I started charging up the knoll.

"Uh, not really," they said, moments after I had arrived beside their tent.

"Oh, I think there's enough space here for me, actually," I said, dropping my pack and yanking my tent out.

"Oh, well. OK." There were a few murmured words and some rustling.

I flashed my light around 360 degrees and went back to setting up my tent. "I think I've been followed by a mountain lion for the last half an hour or so."

"Oh my God," said a woman's voice. "We've been hearing something outside our tent all night."

"It stopped about forty-five minutes ago. That was why I called to you. I thought maybe you'd been making the noises," the man added by way of explanation.

"Definitely not me. Probably the same lion though. Thanks for letting me camp so close by. I think it has a territorial boundary down there."

"Sure thing. We'll probably sleep better now."

"Me too. And I'll try and be very quiet when I leave in the morning."

DAY 32 / 44 MILES

"Perhaps choosing a zebra print for lion country was a bad idea."

I laughed at my own joke. After all, I had passed by the majority of thru-hikers at this point. There wasn't really anyone else to talk to. I savored the conversations I had already had, replaying them in my mind to keep me company. When I got tired of that, I talked to myself.

I clambered over a fallen log and, with my first stride on the other side, felt a twinge run down my left leg. My gait became a limp, and then a hobble. I realized that I'd pulled something—likely a hamstring. Stopping to palpate the back of my thigh, I noted there were no bulges, and no heat. Just stiffness. I tried to touch my toes, but I couldn't even touch my kneecaps. The musculature of my left leg had seized. Slipping my pack off, I sat down, awkwardly contorting myself to accommodate the tightness that had developed. I pulled out my first-aid kit, which was nothing more than sports tape, triple antibiotic ointment, and a handful of ibuprofen in a plastic baggie. For the second time on my hike thus far, I took an ibuprofen and got back to my feet. Within twenty minutes the pain had subsided, even though I still limped slightly. *It's marvelous how effective 200 mg of vitamin I is when my body is unaccustomed to it!*

The mixed Jeffrey and sugar pine forest was stifling. As I climbed, not even a whisper of air moved through the bushes and shrubs of the understory. Near the junction with the summit trail to Butt Mountain I heard voices before a family of four appeared on the trail, descending toward me. Some miles later I saw a cement post ahead of me. I recognized it before I reached it. *Halfway. I am halfway through the PCT!* It was worth celebrating, even though it had taken me over a month. I was barely keeping up with Scott's pace—not breaking it—and it was taking every last ounce of mental and physical strength I had.

CHAPTER 22
LASSEN VOLCANIC NATIONAL PARK, CALIFORNIA

DAY 33 / 45 MILES

I was still in California, which made it hard to believe that I'd crossed into the volcanic Cascade Range, the mountains that extended all the way home. The day before, I had circled around the first volcano— Lassen Peak—on trails comprised of decidedly volcanic soil. The loose, ashy sand, sprinkled with chunks of pumice, reassured me that I was indeed leaving the granitic Sierra behind and passing into a new landscape—even if I had yet to cross a state border. It was a bit like starting out at a trailhead, another place of beginnings.

At a trailhead, it is frequently difficult to see more than a few feet down the trail. Likewise on the Pacific Crest Trail, I could never know exactly what lay ahead. Even though I had hiked the entire PCT before, I did not know what the trail conditions ahead of me were like, what the weather would be, or how many logs I would clamber over in frustration. I couldn't know how many heart-stopping wildlife encounters lay between me and the end of this trip. It was this promise of something new and unknown—this tantalizing mystery—that fueled my addiction. I was desperate for discovery. Perhaps curiosity was why, feeling dead in a well-ordered life, I had left it behind to roam all those years ago—and kept returning.

Now, the pursuit of a record was providing yet another avenue for exploration. When the southern terminus of the PCT stood there, offering the chance for adventure, I was compelled to accept, despite my fear. I was constantly intrigued by how my body continued, without proper fuel or adequate rest, to function over the course of my journey. Sometimes I felt like I was following a stranger on an arduous pilgrimage. *When will I break? Will I? How much is too much?*

At the beginning, I had no way of knowing exactly what lay ahead on the most demanding hike of my life. I was glad that I hadn't. Yet, despite the hardships, I remained fascinated with the search for an answer to those questions, and this one: *Can I do this?*

My pack was light as I pounded out the miles as fast as I could. My hamstring still hindered me, but I ignored it. Instead I focused on maintaining my range of motion and not compensating my stride in ways that could lead to additional injury. I was logging over forty miles every day now and I didn't plan to stop. My body, amazingly, seemed to have surpassed athleticism and become a machine. When I was awake, I walked. When I stopped, I slept. There was not much else. Its operation often seemed to be on autopilot. But there was a deeper meaning behind this sleep, eat, walk mechanism. It meant that it was no longer my body that was most likely to fail—only my mind could stop me now. *Can it handle the loneliness, the lack of sleep, the unrelenting drive necessary to cover another thirteen hundred miles in less than a month?*

"Calories in, miles out," I mumbled, chewing on a stale bar. My stomach had started to turn at the thought of eating another energy bar, another Oreo, or more prunes. But I needed the nutrition to keep going—at this point I couldn't stop early if I wanted to match the record, much less break it. I wished I hadn't let the air out of the packaging on some of my supplies to make more room in the boxes.

Food is fuel. Only calories matter. It was my only mantra. I said it aloud, I said it in my head.

I thought of when my stomach had gone south during ultramarathons and I could not eat. Not here, I could not choose the bonk over the goal. *I must eat. I must go forward. There is no stopping until Canada.* I had become focused on the goal to the exclusion of all else. Walking, eating, and sleeping were just means to my end. They were what would get me there. *My body is a machine and I must give it energy to carry on.*

In my tent that night, I dumped out the remains of my food bag: three Oreos, a packet of almond butter, two tortillas, a snack bag of M&M's, three energy bars, and an ounce of coconut oil. I was forty-five miles from Burney Falls State Park where my next resupply box sat. My laminated town guide told me they closed at 6 p.m.

I smeared the almond butter on one tortilla and laid the Oreos end to end in the middle. I topped it with the remaining coconut oil. It was a desperation meal, but it would have to do. Tomorrow, I would turn thirty-two. Rather than cake, my birthday gift to myself would be cranking out miles faster, and on fewer calories, than I had yet done on this trail.

How will my body do it?

I'd follow myself down the trail the next day and find out.

CHAPTER 23
SHASTA-TRINITY NATIONAL FOREST, CALIFORNIA

DAY 35 / 49 MILES

Snow-clad Mount Shasta towered in the distance. Pausing in the cool morning air to admire the mountain, I imagined that she was wishing me a happy birthday welcome to the Cascades. For the next several hours, I hustled across the waterless Hat Creek Rim. A well-known escarpment among thru-hikers, it was the first thirty-mile waterless stretch since the desert. Hat Creek Rim would be hot by midday and I wanted to get across it as quickly as I could. Thinking about anything and everything and nothing, I focused on moving as fast as I could with my nearly empty pack.

The shadows of late afternoon were starting to grow as I plunged down the side trail leading to the Burney Falls State Park store. It was 5 p.m. I'd made it with an hour to spare. The picnic tables outside were littered with packs, empty food packages, and thru-hikers. Among them was a face I knew from hiker get-togethers over the preceding years—Pringles.

It was the first familiar face I'd seen in over one thousand miles, since Hiker Heaven. I threw my pack down on the table where he and several others sat before running inside to get my box.

"So, my partner is meeting me in Ashland and I'm going to try and mash some big miles to get there ASAP," Pringles proclaimed as I devoured a bag of chips, a can of bean dip, and some ice cream. "I thought I'd hike with you for as long as I can. Maybe all the way there. What do you think?"

"Sure. I would love the company. I plan to be there in five days. Forty-five miles per day."

"Let's do it! When's your next resupply?"

"Ammirati's in two days. Then, Seiad Valley."

"Got it."

"Four or five more miles today. Are you ready?"

I threw my empty resupply box in the trash and headed back up the hill to the PCT while Pringles said goodbye to his friends. He fell into stride behind me and, for the first time in nearly fifteen hundred miles, I was walking in conversation with someone else. He howled as we followed the trail over the dam at the outlet to Lake Britton. I joined him.

DAY 37 / 50 MILES

It was strange to have a companion, yet hiking with Pringles was easy. He didn't complain about the lack of breaks or long miles, even though I could tell it was hard for him to hike farther than his typical thirty miles per day.

"Dammit!"

I turned around to see Pringles standing with one foot in the air. Near him, a flattened cow pie full of wriggling maggots sat in the middle of the trail—with a large footprint in the middle of it.

"Oh my God . . . " I was at once horrified for him—the patty had oozed around his shoe on impact and cow shit was covering the entire sole and upper—and morbidly amused.

"This isn't funny!"

"I'm sorry. I know. I just . . . " I doubled over, laughing the pent-up laughter of someone who'd been taking life far too seriously for too many miles.

Pringles picked up a stick and scraped as much off as he could. I managed to bring my laughter under control.

"It's dry air here. I'm sure most of it will fall off before we get to camp. I'm sorry that happened."

"Yeah. These are not going inside the tent tonight. Or ever again."

"I don't blame you."

As we continued on, I felt an immense sense of well-being. I realized just how much I had needed to laugh—hard. Sipping on my water, I glanced at the Halfmile app. We were almost to the next spring. It was a good thing, too, as I only had a few sips left. Northern California had been hotter and drier than I'd anticipated.

"Uh oh . . . "

Pringles's voice got my attention and I looked up. The slope ahead of us was wet and muddy—trampled by cows. One cow was lying on its back in the spring . . . legs straight up in the air. The stench emanating from its dead, bloated body was nauseating.

"So, I think we'll skip this water source," I commented. With bandannas over our noses, we ran to get past it.

DAY 38 / 45 MILES

"I don't have enough food to keep hiking with you. I'm going into Etna."

With that declaration, Pringles sat down in the parking lot at Etna Summit. He was nearly mad with hunger. I knew the feeling well.

"OK. Do you think you'll get a ride this late?" Situated on a nearly deserted road, the hitch into Etna was notoriously hard.

He shrugged.

"Here, take this," I said, digging a tuna packet out of my pack and handing it to him. "In case you have to wait a while."

We said goodbye and I crossed the road. When I glanced back, he was already devouring it. *There goes my dinner.* My stomach growled, but I ignored it.

The trail was soft as I climbed up, the evening light illuminating the gently rolling ridgelines of the Marble Mountains. It had been strange at first to have another person walking behind me. Now it seemed strange to walk alone.

I kicked a pinecone down the trail in front of me. Company had been a nice distraction, but it had also been draining. I'd grown accustomed to hiking in silent meditation. Now that it had returned, silence felt like a blanket I could cuddle into. My phone beeped, its sound loud and foreign in the woods. I pulled it out of my pocket, surprised that I had reception and that it was off airplane mode.

"I'm eating a cheeseburger and drinking beer! I don't regret leaving the trail AT ALL!"

I turned my phone off and put it back in my pack. I was glad Pringles had gotten into town, but now I wished I hadn't given him my dinner.

CHAPTER 24

KLAMATH NATIONAL FOREST, CALIFORNIA

DAY 39 / 50 MILES

Gripping my hips, I leaned into the climb. I was vaguely aware that the fingertips of each hand now almost touched each other, meaning I'd lost even more weight. The extent to which my body had changed over the course of the hike continued to fascinate me. Since the High Sierra, I'd also found I could breathe through my nose even while climbing steep grades. I was lost in those thoughts when a movement on the trail ahead startled me and I jumped.

"Hi!" I said.

"Hi." He had wild curls barely contained by a buff and was standing awkwardly in the middle of the trail—a bit like a surprised bear.

"So, are you NoBo?" I asked, using hiker slang for a northbound thru-hiker. From his wild beard and dirt-stained clothes I already knew the answer.

"Yeah. My name's Tao."

My question seemed to reassure him that I wasn't a ghost, at least not the kind to be concerned about.

"Same. I'm Anish."

He stepped aside and fell into stride behind me. We chatted easily and after twenty minutes he asked where I was headed for the day.

"Seiad Valley."

I could tell by his silence that there was some math taking place. It was 1 p.m. and Seiad was still twenty-five miles away. It was going to be fifty full miles for me and, once again, I regretted stopping early the night before.

"Mind if I hike there with you?"

"Not at all." I was surprised, but happy to have some company again.

Tao was quieter than Pringles, but his conversation was thoughtful and philosophic. Its in-depth provocativeness distracted me from the monotony of the trail through the Northern California forest.

"There's something about thru-hiking . . . living out here. It makes you feel alive in a way that nothing else can. Know what I mean?" Tao asked, stopping to take in the view of a waterfall cascading down the rocks next to the trail.

"Absolutely."

Hours of hiking later, we popped out onto a deserted paved road paralleling the massive Klamath River. It was still six miles into town and the sky was already dark. I was completely out of food and wanted nothing more than the resupply box waiting for me at the RV park—or that pack of tuna I'd given Pringles. Tao and I walked side by side in a stupefied silence borne out of fatigue and hunger. After the first mile along the road, he began to slow and I pulled ahead quickly. Soon, I was falling asleep as I walked—weaving across the deserted road. I snapped back awake.

"Walk faster, you'll stay awake," I told myself. Tao's light was a speck behind me now.

I wondered if he'd stop alongside the road and sleep. He'd sounded determined to hike his first forty-mile day seven hours ago. I knew first-hand that the drive to accomplish a goal could overpower many weaknesses, but it was up to Tao whether he would allow it to do so.

It was almost 10 p.m. when I crossed the river. In lieu of calories, frustration fueled my legs. Doubting that anyone would be around at the campground when I got there, I decided to run. Three strides later

I went back to walking at four miles per hour. My body was adapted to one thing only—running was a completely foreign movement now.

I reached the RV park in Seiad Valley at 10:45 p.m., surprised to see that lights were still on. I walked up the gravel drive to the office door and twisted the handle. It was locked. A button next to the door informed me that I could ring for help until 11 p.m. Feeling guilty for the late hour—but desperate for food—I pushed it.

"Hi. What can I do for you?"

"Hi," I spoke into the speaker hesitantly, "Well, I'm thru-hiking the PCT and I know it's late, but I just wondered if I could tent camp tonight . . . and I have a box here. Heather Anderson."

"I'll be right there."

Moments later a man appeared from another building. He seemed completely unconcerned that a filthy woman in a ragged zebra sundress was standing on his porch at 11 p.m. He unlocked the door and I followed him inside. My box—clad in its easily recognizable purple duct tape and Care Bear stickers—was sitting alone on the counter.

"Been expecting you," he said, smiling. He slid my box toward me. "You can pitch your tent wherever you want out front. Shower and laundry?"

"Yes, but in the morning." I handed him the cash for a tent site, shower, and laundry.

He nodded. "That's fine. The bathhouse is right behind this one."

"There's another hiker. He's not too far behind me. I think he's planning to come here tonight, unless he stopped along the road."

"No problem. Tell him that he can pay in the morning."

He turned off all the lights behind us and I walked back down the gravel drive. The soft, grassy lawn was inviting me to sleep for far more than five hours. I selected a spot and began setting up my tent. No sooner had I finished than a headlamp appeared, coming up the drive.

"Tao! You made it! Forty miles. Congratulations!"

Tao's smile was both weary and elated as he stood there leaning on his trekking poles. I knew exactly how he felt.

"The owner said you can pay in the morning. Nice work getting here."

"Thanks for pulling me along with you today. I can't believe you do that every single day." He slipped his pack off and began to set up his own camp.

"You're welcome. But really, you did all the work."

I crawled into my tent and fell asleep listening to the serenade of crickets and the murmuring Klamath River.

DAY 40 / 37 MILES

I ripped my dress off over my head, eager for my first shower in six hundred miles. I shrieked in surprise at the sight of my naked body, the first glimpse I'd had of it since the Saufley's. Every rib was prominent. I turned slowly in front of the mirror. My shoulder blades were just that—blades. I wondered how my clothing had not been sliced to ribbons. Every knob of my spine stuck out in sharp relief. I was gaunt above the waist, yet my quads and hamstrings bulged with powerful muscles. Chiseled calves flexed as I turned to observe my reflection. Nascent dreads crowned my head, looking more like Medusa than Marley.

I stepped out of the shower and dried off with paper towels. Every last thing I owned needed to be washed, but I had to wear something while I did laundry. I inventoried what lay on the floor. My dress: disgusting. Wool base layers: ripe. My bra, wind shirt, and three pairs of socks: all coated with dirt and sweat. The only remotely clean thing was my stretchy buff headwrap.

"Not much choice." I picked up the wool pants that hadn't been washed for thirteen hundred miles and pulled them on. The waist sagged nearly to my crotch, stopped only by my hips. In fact, the only place they still fit was over my calf muscles.

"I wonder . . . " I yanked the pants off and picked up the buff. Stepping into it, I wiggled the buff upward until it became the tightest, shortest miniskirt I'd ever worn. But it fit. I threw my wind shirt on and gathered up the rest of my clothes to put into the washing machine. I was going to walk into Oregon that night completely clean.

CHAPTER 25
CRATER LAKE NATIONAL PARK, OREGON

DAY 43 / 48 MILES

I retraced my steps along the highway, heading back to the trail after resupplying at Mazama Village. The sun slanted much lower in the sky at 6 p.m. than it had at the start of my hike. Summer was ebbing as I hiked to northern latitudes. And, yet again, I was behind schedule for the day because it was so hard to drag myself away from resupply points. The lure of endless calories within easy reach, a shower, laundry, a bench or chair to sit on—they were all too much to turn away from. At least this time I had managed to skip the shower and laundry, instead using paper towel, soap, and water from the sink to quickly scrub down the important areas.

Now I was heading into a section of trail that was unfamiliar to me, and I'd have to hike through all of it in the dark. Despite having hiked across Oregon twice before, I had never taken the official PCT through Crater Lake National Park. Like almost every other thru-hiker, I had followed the stunning alternate along the actual rim of the high, deep-blue lake. I only knew the official PCT as a squiggle traversing shallow topo lines on the map. But setting a record required hiking the official route.

"It will be flat and fast," I told myself. I shifted my pack as I turned off the highway and onto the trail. "Ugh, so heavy." The hike out of Mazama Village was always miserable, requiring a gallon of water and several days of food, no matter the pace.

It was hard to believe I had been here only one year ago, lost in the fog. I'd been grieving the end of a relationship—two relationships really—my dissolved marriage and a more recent breakup.

Back then as I followed the alternate route at the rim's edge, the fog had thickened and combined with the lingering snow on the ground to create a whiteout effect. With night approaching, I was unable to see anything but swirling whiteness. I felt like I was floating, with no up or down, right or left, forward or behind. *Somewhere I have to turn left and find the trail again. But where do I leave the road?* There were no signs on this PCT alternate. The eeriness of walking the edge of an ancient caldera seeped into my bones. I was scared. *Deep breaths . . . deep breaths. You're warm. You're on a road. You're OK. You won't get lost.*

I wanted nothing more than to find my way back into the forest where I felt safe—far from the unseen lake. I was angry that I was even there, lost in fog when I should have been back in my life with a partner, an apartment, and a job. When my partner of six months had left I'd discovered that I couldn't bring myself to stay in my existence there either. I knew it was an empty life with or without him, yet I resented being driven to the trail under those circumstances. A nearby plain looked vaguely familiar, so I rambled off of the road, wandering deeper into the fog. Realizing my stupidity, I turned around and luckily found my way back. Having nearly become completely lost, I half expected will-o'-the-wisps to appear next, luring me into the woods as darkness fell. I had no choice but to camp where I was, while I was still "found."

I pitched my tent in a clear space beneath a lone whitebark pine. Its gnarled silhouette seemed to echo the heartbroken loneliness I felt after being left. I burrowed into my bag, trying to stay warm and ignore the eerie fog creeping around my camp. The sloped ground made it difficult to fall asleep quickly.

I was jolted awake at 2 a.m. by the low growl of thunder. Opening the vestibule of my tent, I surveyed the moonlit landscape, now fog-free, around me. I was high and exposed, and the lone tree above my camp put me at extreme risk for lightning strikes. To the east, flashes illuminated the sky. I crawled back into my bag and planned for the approaching storm. First, I set my shoes side by side so they'd be easy to slip on. If the lightning got too close for comfort, I'd grab my sleeping pad, dash for the ditch across the road, and squat on the pad. Plan in place, I laid back with my eyes closed. The flashes penetrated my eyelids and I counted the seconds before the accompanying thunder. *4. 5. 7. 7. 7. 8. 10. 10. 20. . . .* The storm was moving away.

A radiant sunrise woke me at 5 a.m. I broke camp rapidly, musing on how the weather along the edge of Crater Lake the day before had echoed my internal turmoil. Like the fog that made the world vanish, now my tears obliterated everything as I grieved. I'd been wandering, completely lost, but somehow I had found a way through both. Still, underneath it all, lay my anger at loss and heartbreak—flashing and growling like a distant storm. But that morning, under unbridled sunshine, I felt like something magical had transpired inside of me. The sadness that had clouded my mind for weeks was gone and the anger I felt had dissipated. I felt free—unburdened—and ready to take back control of the direction of my life.

All packed up, I finally turned to look at the lake, to face its bittersweet memories full on. I was surprised to see that it was not a shimmering sapphire. Instead, it was lead gray and dead. *A good place to leave heartache.* I turned my back on it, looking north. Ahead, the forests, peaks, and valleys of my future were aglow with golden dawn.

I walked.

One year after that fateful trip, I was thankful the official PCT did not follow the rim of Crater Lake. I wasn't ready to face it again, even during the terra incognita of night. I did not want to bring that sorrow into the midst of this thru-hike. Still it was hard to forget that I'd come here to grieve a boyfriend I'd loved and lost as I walked the rim. Nor could I forget that even longer ago, I'd hiked in the moonlight along the lakeshore with my now ex-husband on our first thru-hike. Crater Lake held five trillion gallons of water—and a seemingly equal measure of my heart's memories. It was a place of subterranean destructive power, where a mountain had once dissolved into an explosive cloud of ash. But it was also a place of healing. The epitome of sacred Earth, it was Shiva-like—both creator and a destroyer.

Now, as I hiked the official PCT route through Crater Lake National Park, mosquitoes thronged my sweaty body. My shoulders ached and the sores on my lower back—caused long ago by the bear canister—were raw and stinging from sweat. I picked up sticks and placed them along my spine to alleviate the pressure from my pack. They afforded only a modicum of relief.

I had made sure to carry plenty of water, remembering that the alternate route had an extended waterless stretch. Now I crossed meadows and streams over and over again. Pulling out my map, I saw that creeks flowed across the route at regular intervals. Anger and frustration rose up inside me. *Why didn't I actually think about what I was doing instead of going off of remembered patterns? Why am I carrying three quarts of water?* I thought about dumping it out to save energy, but then I'd just have to get more from a stream later, which would probably waste the equivalent in time.

I climbed over a fallen log . . . and another . . . and another. The forest—with only half of its members still vertical—seemed to be at a stalemate in its war with gravity. The downed trees, littered across a flat, open landscape, also made it difficult to decipher the course of the trail. My heavy pack swayed back and forth as I traversed the jungle gym, climbing and ducking.

The Halfmile app did not show waypoints or mileages for this stretch. I only knew it was sixteen miles between where the official trail diverged from the alternate and Grouse Hill, where they came back together. I assumed the data was missing for good reason. *Who the hell would hike this practically unmaintained trail?* I tried to guess which creek I was crossing. *Perhaps this is Bybee Creek? Or maybe it is this one?*

Eleven p.m. came and went, escorted by frustration. My glacial pace was robbing me of any hope of making it to Red Cone Spring for the night. No grief or thunderstorms, but I gave in to weariness and conceded defeat. I set up my tent and crawled inside.

CHAPTER 26
MOUNT THIELSEN WILDERNESS, OREGON

DAY 44 / 54 MILES

Morning came as it always did—too soon. For a second when I awoke, I didn't remember what I was in the midst of. Then a wave of utter exhaustion rolled over me. My eyelids were caked with grit. My nose was congested and my eyeballs were hot from dehydration. Groping for my drinking tube, I downed an entire liter, thankful, in that moment, for the overabundance of water I had lugged from Mazama the night before. I rolled over and picked up my maps, squinting at them through barely open eyes: Day 44, fifty miles to Windigo Pass. *It's good to have goals, but I sincerely wish I could see a number less than forty for once.* The truth was, as long as I kept logging fifty miles a day across Oregon I would tie the record. Washington—with its bigger climbs and descents—would be like hitting a brick wall after the gentle terrain of Northern California and Oregon. I anticipated my mileage dropping back to forty when I got there. To actually break the record, I'd have to go farther each day. Yet, I doubted I would have any reserves left for a strong final push. In addition to the fatigue, my body had begun to feel wrong in a way I'd never experienced and couldn't pinpoint.

I broke camp and found that it was easier to follow the trail through the jumble of pick-up sticks in the daylight. Soon the debris lessened, and I entered open pumice flats. By the time I reached Red Cone Spring at 9 a.m., it was already hot in the glaring sun. A huge water cache lay under a tarp near the junction with the alternate trail coming down off the rim of the lake. I peeked underneath at the dozens of jugs. It seemed superfluous for them to be here, so close to Red Cone Spring. Curiosity satisfied, I dropped the tarp and hiked on. A few hours later, I reached Thielsen Creek and sat down next to another hiker who was already filtering his water.

"I ran out on that climb. I'm so thirsty!" I commented, dropping purification tablets into my water bladder.

"Would you like some of my filtered water?"

"No, thank you though. I can wait."

"It's really no big deal. I have a Sawyer filter. It's easy." He poured some water from his bottle into my empty one. I didn't argue and plopped an electrolyte tablet in. While it fizzed, I watched him scoop more water into his bladder, screw the Sawyer filter onto the top, and then squeeze the water into his bottle.

"That's pretty slick! Do you like it?" I'd never seen a filtration system so light or simple that involved no pumping.

"Yeah, I love it."

Chugging the ice cold water, I thought briefly about Mark, who'd given me the chlorine tablets at Phantom Ranch so many years ago. *I wonder if he's discovered Sawyer yet.*

"I'm Flip-Flop," said the other hiker as he put his filter away and picked up his pack.

"Anish."

We fell into step and he walked behind me.

"How'd you get your name?" I asked. He wore regular shoes.

"Oh, I'm doing a flip-flop hike from Ashland."

"Ah, that makes sense."

I hadn't expected to see many thru-hikers this far north so early in the season. Seeing someone completing their single-season hike in a nonlinear fashion—starting somewhere in the middle and hiking to one end before going back and hiking the other way—made more sense. It was nice to hike with someone again. Flip-Flop was fast and we blazed down the trail, winding along ridges at a fast clip. He talked nonstop, which was a great distraction from the miles even if I wasn't computing much of it. As the terrain rolled on, my mind wandered to when I was on this section of trail a year ago. It had been mostly snow covered then.

"We're coming to a junction soon. Stay right," Flip-Flop said, looking at his GPS.

We came to a saddle where the trail took a sharp left. A sign on a tree pointed right and read "PCT," but I barely paused. We hiked faster as the trail began to descend because the mosquitoes were thickening. Soon a creek emerged on the right and we wound down to cross it. My stomach churned. There wasn't supposed to be water until an off-trail spring, eight miles away.

"Halfmile didn't mention this creek," I said, "Although, I suppose there have been quite a few he hasn't mentioned here and there. I'm going to top off."

Flip-Flop stopped too. We both refilled our water as quickly as possible while swatting at the clouds of mosquitoes. A quarter of a mile later we reached a trailhead parking lot. Instantly my gut feeling was confirmed: we'd gone the wrong way. Without stopping I turned around—a weathered sign on a nearby tree said "PCT 2 miles."

Although I knew it was not a sustainable pace I tore back up the trail at well over three miles per hour. I heard Flip-Flop's gasping as he tried to keep up. In my mind all I could think of was the thirteen more miles I'd already had to do to reach Windigo Pass. Now I was adding four more. A fifty-four-mile day. Back at the saddle, breathless, I searched for our mistake. Now, it was obvious there was a faint trail going straight across the saddle. A low-hanging tree branch had shielded the trail tread and trail markers from our view. The much more defined path to Miller Lake Trailhead seemed to be what the ancient sign that read, "Windigo Pass" was indicating. It was a mistake anyone could have made.

I hiked along the PCT at top speed. Flip-Flop continued on with me for about thirty more minutes.

"I'm going to stop here."

"OK. Nice to meet you. Have a good hike." I was too pissed and stressed to slow down for anything. I didn't even pause.

An hour or so later, I commanded myself to back off. I was burning through mental and physical energy that I didn't have to spare. Taking several deep breaths, I counseled myself to recalibrate.

"What happened, happened. Nothing I can do now will change it. Stop wasting mental energy and just move forward. One step in front of the other."

It was midnight when I at last reached Windigo Pass.

DAY 45 / 48 MILES

At Willamette Pass I sat down on a log and pulled off my shoes and socks to air out my sweaty, reeking feet. I ate some dried fruit and drank a little water before reaching down to put my socks back on. I stared at my right foot. Where the blister had been in the desert, there was now nothing but black flesh and white, sloughing skin. My stomach clenched and I felt ice-cold despite the 80-degree heat: my foot was rotting.

It reminded me of the blood infection I got—from stepping on a fence wire—a few days before leaving for the Grand Canyon. I had ignored it for two days before the swollen red lines running up my leg forced me to go to the emergency room. There, the doctor had lanced my foot without any anesthetic. I held perfectly still, clinging tightly to the armrests, but it was excruciating.

"Doesn't that hurt?" my mom had asked, wincing.

I clenched my jaw tightly and said nothing, my knuckles white from gripping the armrests of the chair.

"It certainly does. She's tough," the doctor had said, setting down the lance and swabbing the newly cleaned wound.

Now, I picked up a stick and bravely inserted it into the black hole. I twisted, and a gob of loose flesh came out. Using my pocketknife, I excavated deeper and deeper into my foot. I dug out giant scoops of dead skin packed with dirt. A quarter of an inch into the calloused flesh, I hit soft, pink skin—healthy and new. There was no pus. I continued widening the hole. When all of the detritus was removed, I was able to see that my foot was not actually rotting or gangrenous. Rather, the cycle of blistering and callousing had formed thick layers of dead skin packed with black dirt that had created the illusion of black, rotting flesh.

"Oh thank God. It's not rotting."

I filled the hole with antibiotic ointment, taped over it, and put my socks and shoes back on.

Climbing again, I passed the chain of Rosary Lakes as they shrunk in size before winding down and along a ridge with peekaboo views of Waldo Lake—massive even in the distance. The rolling terrain of southern and central Oregon was not difficult, but it was rather monotonous. Ridge, lake, plain, lake . . . I knew that it wasn't far to my intended campsite near Charlton Lake, but the viewless, predominantly coniferous woods made it seem like an eternity. Mosquitoes came out at nightfall and I hustled through the darkness, pushing past the spur trails leading to the excellent camping by the lake, opting instead for a semi-flat spot covered in branches and debris right next to the trail.

The cavity in my foot had been a baseless scare, but one of my toes was still unnaturally feverish and swollen. There were no visible wounds, yet it acted like it was badly infected. I had gone from a forty-mile-a-day rock star in a zebra dress to a fifty-mile-a-day supernova that burned white-hot and fast. Yet, I couldn't help but feel that my body was beginning to collapse in on itself—following an inevitable, spiraling route into a black hole.

CHAPTER 27

THREE SISTERS WILDERNESS, OREGON

DAY 46 / 49 MILES

The air smelled strongly of campfire, yet I hadn't passed any camps in the five hours I'd been hiking since that morning. My gut warned me of something far more urgent—that it wasn't campfire at all but the forest itself that was burning. I hiked faster in a panic from an unknown conflagration, threatening from somewhere unseen. Its specter continued to follow me through the abandoned wilderness—water sources were dry or reduced to puddles now thick with mosquito larvae and pollen. *Dry land. Smoke. Fire.* I felt like an animal trapped in a world that was about to end—or desiccated tinder waiting to ignite. I wondered if chronic dehydration was the reason behind the hollow feeling that permeated my bones. *Am I dying? What's wrong with me?* I hadn't had any water since the morning. There was a general feeling of unwellness hovering beneath the surface, even as I continued to plow through the miles—I just couldn't place my finger on it. My arms, my kidneys, and my joints all ached in an unfamiliar way. I sensed I was nearing the limit of what my body could handle.

Through the trees to my left I saw a wide-open meadow. Memory, anticipation, and fear battled inside of me—I remembered finding a crystal clear, spring-fed creek snaking across this meadow the year before. *Will it be there this year, as dry as it is? Is this the right meadow? Where is the fire?* I bounded into the glade, running toward the edge of the streambed that sliced across the middle. As I drew closer, I could see sunlight bouncing off water as it rolled across the vale. I dropped to my knees and scooped palmfuls into my mouth.

The creek was only about two inches deep—a fraction of its depth from the prior year—but it was flowing. I drank until I shivered in the hot sun. Then I filled my water bottles and bladder.

It was midafternoon when I stepped onto the pumice flat called Wickiup Plain. The view of the mountains stopped me in my tracks. South Sister appeared ahead of me in flaming red glory, contrasting with the darker rock of Middle and North Sisters in the distance. My heart swelled with the beauty of this landscape dominated by towering volcanos that soared to over ten thousand feet. I crossed the plain rapidly—spurred by thirst. Each footfall sent puffs of pumice powder into the air. The easy tread allowed me to gaze up at the redheaded mountain while I walked. For some unknown reason, I had always felt a powerful spiritual connection to South Sister deep in my soul. If I could, I would never leave this spot, so as to spend my life in adoration of this one mountain. Unlike Mazama—whose eruption gave us Crater Lake—South Sister's power seemed benevolent. I felt safe and happy here.

When I reached the next snaking stream, this one deeper, I dropped to my knees, stuck my face into the icy flow, and let the water fill my mouth. I'd run out of chlorine tabs that morning, but it didn't matter. It would be two weeks before I'd come down with giardiasis, and by then I'd be done—I hoped.

With a belly full of spring water, I rolled onto my back and yanked off my shoes and socks. My left pinky toe was still hot, red, and swollen. I palpated it again, seeking the injury that had led to the infection, but once again found nothing. I plunged my feet into the creek, wincing as they lost feeling. I exhaled and relaxed, gazing at the mountain.

After a few minutes, I pulled my feet out, rinsing my socks in the rushing water before slipping them back on. I could still feel the injured toe. I yanked the sock back off and wrung it out more thoroughly. Setting the sock in the sun, I slathered some antibiotic ointment on the flushed and puffy toe. Even though no wound was visible, I figured it wouldn't hurt.

I stretched back out on the grass, closed my eyes, and listened to the birds, the gurgle of the water, and the rustle of the occasional breeze in the nearby pines. I became aware of the texture of the ground I was lying on—lumps and rocks pushing into my back. I felt the faint tickle of ants and other insects wandering along my bare legs. Gradually I also felt the presence of the red mountain standing above me, overseeing her queendom.

After an eternity of bliss, I picked up my phone. I was shocked to see that I'd been lying there for forty-five minutes. After pulling my sock and my shoes on, I thrust my face in the water, drinking as much as I could hold. Then I filled my bottles and bladder for the long carry northward as I headed uphill, off of the Wickiup, and toward the lava fields that awaited me.

Darkness fell before I had finished traversing the slopes of the Three Sisters. The full moon rose, drenching the sparse forest and open terrain in silver light. I clicked off my headlamp and hiked by lunar illumination alone. The less I relied on my eyes, the more acute my hearing became—I heard the deafening cascade of Obsidian Falls long before I glimpsed its ghostly veil. At the top of the climb, I was wonderstruck by the moonlit glimmer of volcanic glass on the ground around me—black diamonds scattered at my feet.

CHAPTER 28
WILLAMETTE NATIONAL FOREST, OREGON

DAY 47 / 42 MILES

I walked along the soft, pine needle-covered trail dappled with late morning sunshine. My arms and shoulders ached more today, especially my triceps. I massaged them gently while I walked, to no avail. I didn't remember doing anything to them. It wasn't overuse from trekking poles, since I didn't carry them. This was a strange, dull, deep aching—as though an animal was gnawing at my flesh from the inside. Without warning, my knees buckled under me and I faceplanted in the dirt, hitting my head hard.

I wasn't injured, but I lay there unmoving anyway. The muscles in my thighs twitched rapidly. I wondered if I was indeed being consumed by an animal—me.

"Get up, Anish. C'mon. Get up."

I rolled to the side and stood up, still shaky. *What is happening to me?*

A few miles later I found stones piled on the trail forming a number: "2000." Two thousand miles. No matter that this was my fourth time walking that far, it still amazed me to think that I had actually walked such an astronomical distance—much less at an average of over forty miles per day. A few feet beyond the stones was the trail leading to Big Lake Youth Camp, and my next resupply box. I would have spent more time in wonder at my accomplishment, but I wanted the food that awaited me down the spur trail.

Minutes later, I stood in an air-conditioned office, waiting for someone to find my box. The staff were young, kind, and apparently used to filthy, stinky hikers. They offered me a shower and lunch and use of their computers. I accepted everything gratefully, paying the nominal amount they charged. A woman returned from the back and handed me my box.

"The kids are at their morning activities so you should have the bathhouse to yourself. Girls room is down the hill to the right. Lunch is served promptly at noon, all you can eat. Come back up here anytime to use the computer."

I showered, paying careful attention to my swollen toe and dirty feet. Afterward, I went to the lunch hall, only to discover that it was all-you-can-eat salad. I ate as much as I could hold, but my body still screamed for more calories. On a quiet porch outside an unused building, I unceremoniously upended my box, dumping its contents onto the wooden slats. The same six foods that had filled every box stared up at me: protein powder for dinner, dried fruit, Oreos, coconut oil, granola bars, and sesame snaps. As I pushed them into organized piles, I began to cry uncontrollably. *My body is falling apart! This food has sustained me for two thousand miles, but it's not enough anymore. You gave it a good effort, Anish, but this is the end of the line.* I was being eaten alive—my body cannibalized for protein and energy. This realization had been sudden, but it was undeniably right. A general sense of disease had been growing throughout my fifty-mile-per-day march across Oregon: the aching muscles, the twitching, the falling, the mysteriously inflamed toe . . . it all made perfect sense now. Always strong and resilient, my body was finally hitting its limit, running out of resources, and beginning to fail. I thought about how I'd lost ten pounds in the first ten days, wondering even then if I had enough reserves to make it. The answer was clear now.

I leaned my head back against the building and let my mind drift. *It's over. Everything I've strived for—all the hours of distress, the dehydration,*

the hunger. It's all done. It's all over—the sunrises, the sunsets, the moun-
tains, the nights walking by moonlight, the feeling of power in my body as
I overcame challenges. It's done. No more waterfalls, blue skies, rainbows,
refreshing spring water . . . I just needed to walk over to the road and wait
for a ride into Bend.

Aside from Western States, I had consistently placed high in
hundred-mile ultramarathons, sparking the tiny hope inside me
that kindled into this FKT attempt. I realized now those placements
were obviously due to who had dropped out rather than my abilities.
Obviously. Western States was the only time you've run with the best. And
you barely finished. You're an idiot for basing your perception of yourself
on local races. It's time to accept that you've failed. I'd always been good at
hiking. Now I was going to fall apart and fail to finish a long-distance
hike for the first time. I was not an athlete and never would be.

I woke up, surprised that I had fallen sound asleep in the midst of
my pity party. I looked at the neat piles of food on the deck around me.
They were supposed to feed me all the way to Timberline Lodge—two
and a half days away. *But what about Olallie Lake Resort? I'll pass by*
there tomorrow and I could at least buy a day's worth of food. What if I ate
everything here in the next twenty-four hours? Amazingly, after just a short
nap, my mind was clear and rational, solving problems and rejecting
the old voices and familiar self-destructive thought patterns that always
attacked me at my lowest points.

What if I'm not a failure after all, just slowly starving to death?

I gathered everything into my pack and headed back to the office.
Nearly four hours had passed since I'd arrived—four hours in which
my mind had finally quit, and then rallied to grab hold of hope. I had
known for some time that weakness of mind was the only thing that
could stop me, and it almost had. But there had been a roadblock in my
core—a stubborn will to finish. Whether I failed to break a record or not
was of no consequence: I would not give up.

I sat down at the computer and tried to synthesize the effort of the last
days and hours into words. I'd set up a public Facebook page in order to
provide documentation of my hike because those were the "rules" of the
Fastest Known Time website. At first it had been followed by my family

and friends, which was all I'd ever anticipated. It had since swelled to three thousand people. I didn't know them, but they were there in the back of my mind . . . a lurking audience to either my stunning success or my epic failure. I realized at this point that it didn't matter to me which it was. What mattered was that I was going to try—and keep trying until I was lying in the middle of the trail with no ideas or energy left. It was the process of finding myself that mattered to me, and I believed that this realization might mean something to some of the people who were following along on my journey.

I have been in awe of my body as it has transitioned from athlete into machine. The way it went from barely being able to do 40 miles to cranking them out before 8 p.m. and continuing onward. Now, with only about 600 miles to go I can feel the machine beginning to break down. I sometimes get dizzy, my legs sporadically are weak, my feet have a host of problems and though the end is so close, it still seems so far away and that makes it even harder to push through the miles.

But this I know: I am doing what I was meant to do. What I was born for. Covering miles in the mountains where I feel so much joy. I have cherished every sunrise and sunset for 47 days . . . I cannot think of another time that has happened or will happen again in my life. And nothing will stop me from reaching Canada, whether I break the record or not.

I stood up from the computer and walked back to the PCT. I looked back at the two-thousand-mile stones and smiled. It wasn't over yet.

DAY 48 / 50 MILES

When my watch beeped, I ate one snack. Then another. And another. I felt jet-propelled after plowing through nearly two days' worth of food in one. At the junction with Olallie Lake Resort, I turned and hurried the two-fifths of a mile down to the tiny store on the lake. I walked inside and found far more of a selection than I had expected. On the porch, several hikers and a trail angel ate grapes and apples. I rushed around the store grabbing candy bars, tuna packets, and pop tarts. I wanted to walk out with as many calories as I could carry.

Back on the porch, I couldn't pass up the opportunity to sit and eat with the other thru-hikers. I alternated eating fruit with my newly acquired snacks as I listened to them talk about their hikes—splitting my attention with watching an osprey circle the lake, waiting for a fish. I wasn't supposed to be wasting more time here, but it was so peaceful on the lakeshore that I couldn't resist. After thirty minutes I stood up and said my goodbyes. I had to make it to Timberline Lodge before they closed the next day.

•

CHAPTER 29
MOUNT HOOD NATIONAL FOREST, OREGON

DAY 49 / 50 MILES

The next afternoon I walked into the zoo-like chaos of Timberline Lodge's parking lot and made my way to the store inside the Wy'East building—thirty minutes before they closed. I'd spent the previous couple of hours climbing from the highway in the valley up to the tree line on 11,250-foot Mount Hood, where the eponymous lodge stood. Although Timberline Lodge and the surrounding area was popular with tourists and day hikers, Wy'East was clearly designed with skiers in mind. I hurried past the empty ski racks and closed-up rental closets to the small gift shop. Once again, I'd eaten all of my food. The addition of tuna for dinner and the extra calories of the last few days had stopped the dizzy spells, aching arms, and buckling legs—even my swollen toe seemed better. I collected my box and bought a few extra snacks. Back at the parking lot, in full view of the towering white summit of the stratovolcano, I dumped my food into my backpack and threw away the battered shipping box. *It's only a day to Cascade Locks . . . and Washington. You're almost home.*

Three hours later, I arrived at the alluvial destruction zone of the Sandy River. Two men were camped a short distance away, their tent tucked into a flattish, sandy area clear of the many rocks and uprooted trees that littered the glacial river's wide floodplain. They waved me down and cautioned me not to cross until the morning.

"You can camp here with us. It's too dangerous tonight."

I glanced at their roaring campfire. It was 9:15 p.m. and dusk was gathering. I picked up a sturdy-looking stick from their stockpile of firewood.

"I've gotta give it a try."

At the bank, I stood with my stomach knotted as I watched the roiling, frigid glacial silt, fifteen feet wide. For a second, I was eighteen again and looking down at deep, vast Lake Powell from the edge of a thirty-foot cliff. Others were jumping in and I intended to as well. My stomach was in knots, but then—as now—I tried to be brave.

I thrust the stick into the chocolate milk torrent and nearly toppled over. *It's nearly four feet deep!* I tried again and again, up and downstream, seeking smoother water without deep holes. Finally, I found a spot where it was only up to my mid-thigh, although whitewater broke around partially submerged boulders along my path.

After walking to the edge of the cliff and looking down at Lake Powell, I had known it was time to take back control of my fear of heights. *There is a normal level of fear when confronted with falling into space. There is also irrational fear that can take you over.* Deep breath. Three strides and I had been plummeting.

I stepped into the Sandy River.

Methodically, I worked my way across ten feet of river, plunging the stick as I probed blindly for firm footing. It was nearly dark and the racing water made my eyes swim with vertigo. Reaching the strongest channel of the current, I lifted my right foot to take a step and felt the water grab hold and slowly spin me to face downstream. There— in the never-ending tumult of pounding water disappearing down the flume—I glimpsed my demise. *This is how it ends.*

The water of Lake Powell had been dark and heavy, leaving me oddly suspended in time and space until I located an emerald glimmer above me. Reflexively, my limbs had grasped spasmodically for purchase to take me toward it.

It took everything I had to bring my foot back down to the bottom of the Sandy River in a controlled manner and regain my equilibrium.

I lifted my eyes from the churning and focused on reaching the rocks on the opposite bank, now only five feet away. *Stab, step, stab, step.* I breathed slowly and deeply to keep from shivering as the icy water stripped all my warmth away. *How long have I been in this river? Ten minutes? Three? An hour?* I could no longer feel my legs and feet, but the other side was still just beyond my reach.

Seconds after plunging into Lake Powell, my arms and legs had fallen into sync, every fiber and all my focus on the beckoning shimmer. Arid desert air filled my empty, burning lungs as I burst from the darkness into the light. I was free—exhilarated. With unexpected clarity I understood baptism, the way it felt to conquer fear, and the words: "Take up your mat and walk."

At last, on numb, frozen stubs, I stumbled clumsily up the loose soil on the other side of the Sandy River. Turning, I lifted my arms in triumph. The men on the other side cheered. I threw down my stick, exhausted, and hobbled away.

My feet hurt as though they had been asleep for an eon. The grit in my shoes ground into my feet with such painful intensity that I wasn't sure I could handle it. A half mile later, I stopped, sat on a log, and pulled them off. After changing socks, I scraped as much gravel out of my shoes as I could. Then, I hiked at maximum speed to rebuild the warmth and circulation that my body had lost in the river. Adrenaline from my brush with death spurred me forward. I knew that it was three miles—including a long climb up Bald Mountain—to my camp.

A few yards up the trail I pulled out my treat for the evening—a caffeinated gel. I swallowed it and began to power up the climb, head down. *Switchback, switchback, switchback . . .* As I neared a turn, I glanced up to see cougar eyes illuminated just feet from my face. Unlike my other encounters, I did not recoil or bark defensively. Instead, I lunged forward, arms over my head and I ROARED.

The lion did not pause for a second investigation. It turned tail and fled up the trail, disappearing into the night. Caffeine and adrenaline coursed through my body. I could literally feel the chemicals throbbing in my veins, and I shook with the visceral urge to physically lay hands on the opponent and fight it. I was done being afraid of the night, of lions, of failure—of anything. Chest heaving, I stood and stared in the direction it had gone.

I roared again.

When I had stepped away from the southern terminus fifty days before, it had been the biggest jump of my life. Since then, I'd felt as though I'd been falling the entire time—until that moment when I flung myself into the face of my greatest fear, ready to fight. After fifty days in freefall, I'd landed. I was the lioness now, roaming the day and night fearlessly. Willing to fight anything in my path. To take anything on, whether it be lions in the night or raging glacial rivers or the self-defeating voices that lived in the dark recesses of my own mind. I was now a living incarnation of courage.

I shattered the silent forest with my voice: "NOTHING. WILL STOP ME. FROM GETTING. TO CANADA!!!!"

I hiked onward. The adrenaline flooding my system made my legs feel light. The heady realization that I was no longer controlled by fear had me roaring at every cracking branch or twig. *There is nothing on this mountain that won't know that I am a lioness tonight.*

CHAPTER 30

COLUMBIA RIVER, OREGON— WASHINGTON BORDER

DAY 50 / 38 MILES

Walking through stands of fir in predawn light, it was strange to think that I had once been afraid of heights. It was also strange to awaken to a day where fear of mountain lions and other nocturnal animals seemed silly. *How had I let those fears cage me for so long? What other fears are still hindering me? Can I face each of them bravely and conquer them? Can I harness this courage in every part of my life?*

The Columbia River was so close I could feel it. I hurried along the trail, my breath clouding in front of my face whenever I exhaled. It was the coldest morning yet—a sign I was nearing the end of the line, the north country . . . home.

Ahead of me, I heard the click of poles on rocks. I looked up, startled. There were seldom people moving this early in the morning. A man in shorts—yet also bundled in a hat, gloves, and jacket—approached. He was smiling from ear to ear. I recognized him immediately. After all, we'd hiked over five thousand miles together.

"Remy!" My voice seemed to crack the still air as I ran toward him.

We embraced for a long minute. Then he held my shoulders at arm's length, staring at me.

"Heather! What you're doing is incredible. I knew you could do it."

"Thank you! How is your hike going?"

"Very good! My trail name is Vogue now. Do you have time for a quick break?"

"No, but I'll take one anyway."

We each sat down and pulled something from our packs to eat. In between bites we talked fast, each trying to share months of hiking with one another.

"Southbound is really hard, but I love it. I really think it's the way to hike this trail," Remy said.

"Seems a little early to decide that! The desert in the fall seems like it would be really dry."

"Well, it won't be 110 degrees though."

"True!"

"Where are you headed tonight?"

"Washington. Basically, as far into the state as I can get."

Remy nodded, finishing his snack.

"Remy."

"Yes?"

"Thank you. For everything. And for believing in me, even though this seemed crazy."

"You're welcome, Heather."

I reluctantly stood up. "I have to go."

"I know." He stood up and put on his pack, "Good luck! Stay strong."

We hugged again and I headed north.

"Oh, Heather?"

"What?" I turned to see him smiling at me again.

"I won. I reached the Columbia first."

I laughed as we each continued on our journeys. Divorce is never easy, but it had been the right choice for us. I was happy to have shared a life with him for nearly a decade. I was even happier now that we were each growing and pursuing dreams that made us feel fulfilled—even though we couldn't pursue them together. He might not have understood my drive—I didn't fully understand it yet—but he'd supported my need to pursue a different path and I was grateful.

Earlier, I'd taken a few minutes to read comments on my Facebook page. Most were overwhelmingly positive, but there had been a handful of derisive people who'd read about me somewhere and formed opinions based on their own fears, limitations, misconceptions, and world views. They could not understand me and therefore criticized me. I'd pondered their points, finally coming to the conclusion that I savored my hike in a way that no one else could ever know. Though it had taken me many years, many failed relationships, and many miles of walking, I was finally on the brink of understanding how hiking forty-five to fifty miles per day could be enjoyable. How I could cherish the landscape even as I traversed it so relentlessly.

I'd spent fifty days exploring the tip of the iceberg—90 percent of my self-discovery remained. *But I had to start somewhere.*

At least now I knew that my heart was wedded to the mountains—to the wild places. It was there, and there alone, that I was whole, contented, and blissful. No relationship, career, or wealth could ever take its place. I'd tried that path and found myself empty. Having filled myself with nothing but miles and miles of hiking, I finally understood that it was the beauty of the land that enthralled me so. I would continue to seek more and more—trying to take in as much splendor at once as I could. For that, I was willing to run myself to exhilarated exhaustion over and over again, and yet still crave more.

Hours later I walked across the Bridge of the Gods, spanning the mighty Columbia River. A fountain of joy gushed inside of me, despite the crushing fatigue. *How can I cry so uncontrollably and yet smile so hard at the same time?* I wondered. Fifty days ago, I doubted everything about the feasibility of the goal I'd set for myself. Yet now, the seeming inevitability of achieving it crashed over me like waves borne from deep water. Like the Columbia, visible through the metal slats of the narrow bridge beneath my feet, I was unstoppable.

I had ten days to cover five hundred miles in order to meet the goal I had planned out from the comfort of a couch. If it took me two weeks, I would tie the record of a man I still believed was one of the greatest athletes of all time. I felt like I was in a fairytale, one I was certain to wake up from at any moment. *I can't be doing this.* Yet my feet felt the pavement of Highway 14 through my shoes and my face felt a fine mist as I kissed the sign welcoming me to Washington State. Destiny swelled inside me. Nothing could stop it.

DAY 52 / 49 MILES

I clambered over lava chunks as I hiked through the dark. A year ago, I had been here in deep snow, trying to figure out where the buried trail was without the Halfmile app. Now I was headed to the same camp at Killen Creek on bare trail—in the middle of the night. Whereas before I had been panicked, floundering through snow in fading light to arrive at camp before dark, now, in the pitch black, I was hiking as though it were midday. The beam of my headlamp caught the fog of my breath as it evaporated and made the hoarfrost sparkle. I hustled to stay warm. My memories were vivid, but they were those of another life. I'd been reincarnated.

Rounding a bend, I was greeted with the familiar roar of raging water. I entered the washed-out drainage and picked my way across uneven ridges of loose gravel and glacial sediment deposited by the river's violent outbursts. I slid down some loose sand and scree to the banks of the threaded and tumultuous Adams River. It ran black, cold, and vigorous. I stepped into the first channel.

I didn't scream, although the frigid water shocked me. It swirled up my legs and pushed hard. *"Come with me . . . "* it insisted.

I trudged through water and hobbled onto the opposite side. Water streamed out of my shoes. I winced as my frozen feet made their way to the next channel. Again . . . and again . . . and again. Tears were running down my face when I staggered out of the final torrent, and my teeth chattered hard enough to break. Both feet and legs were a paradoxical mix of numbness and shooting pain. Needing to observe myself remotely, I slipped into a floating state. Outside my own body, away from the pain, I could instruct. I observed the absurdity of my current state without amusement. It was 10:30 p.m. and I was searching the shoulder-high, eroded embankment of a roaring glacial river for anything resembling the resumption of trail. Finally, I found the familiar break in the trees and brush and clawed my way up it. I relied on my hands, digging my fingers into the loose dirt and using exposed roots to pull my struggling lower body over the brink.

When I again stood on solid forested soil—no longer watching myself—I instructed my legs to walk. Now, fully present in my body, I screamed as the thawing sent needle-sharp twinges shooting through every nerve. *Walk, walk, walk. Walk faster to warm up. The pain will stop once you're warm.* My teeth stopped chattering. I paused and looked up. Above me lay the vast ocean of night sky. I breathed deeply, drawing the starlight into my soul. Each time I thought I had reached the outer edges of my ability, some new way to cope rose up from inside me. I forged onward. *You cannot stop.*

"Amazing Grace . . . how sweet the sound . . . that saved a wretch like me . . . " My voice rasped in my parched throat and broke as I chocked on sobs. "I once was lost . . . but now am found . . . "

The ice blocks in my shoes warmed. My voice grew stronger. My legs moved faster.

CHAPTER 31
GOAT ROCKS WILDERNESS, WASHINGTON

DAY 53 / 50 MILES

As I walked through the sunny forest, making my way up into the high alpine of Goat Rocks Wilderness, I thought about my chiropractor. Specifically, a conversation we'd had almost two years ago, when we were unable to pinpoint the cause of an injury that was keeping me from running. He told me that I was an elite athlete—even if I didn't win races—because of the demands that I placed on my body. He recommended rest and dialing back my seventy-five to one-hundred-mile weeks in order to let my body rebound. I'd thanked him for his insight and all the treatments he'd tried, but as I left his office my only thought had been, *I'm not an elite athlete. The people winning races are elites. I'm an average person who needs to lose a few pounds. I just happen to run and hike a lot.* Now, fifty-three days into this hike, I realized that his outside perspective was probably closer to the truth than my internal one. But for some reason, I still didn't feel like an athlete—or at least what I thought it should feel like to be an athlete. I only knew what it was like to be me. *Being me . . .*

I had never been able to accept myself for who I was and, even more so, for who I was not. I was never "normal"—whatever that meant. As a child, I read literature when the rest of my classmates were reading Goosebumps. In high school, I enrolled full-time in community college, earning credits rather than playing sports or partying. In college, I studied day and night, keeping up my grades to retain my scholarships and grants, and worked four part-time jobs to save for the Appalachian Trail. As an adult, I often lost sight of the fact that, to most people, running fifty miles at a time wasn't a normal weekend activity. Nor was knocking off a sixty-five-mile loop on a weekend backpacking trip. Thru-hiking across the country wasn't normal either, much less three times . . . now almost four. It was easy to forget that I approached long distances— distances that 99 percent of people would only consider traveling by a vehicle—as casually as others approached a Sunday matinee.

I broke out above tree line and began to traverse across shrubby slopes. Normalcy still plagued my thoughts. I had backpacked seemingly endless hours since the Mexican border. Despite their difficulty, they had been the best hours of my life. Still, questions rang in my head. *Why am I not like other people I know? Why can't I be happy with the things that made my parents, my friends, and my siblings happy? Marriage, babies, the nine-to-five, a home? Why do I like to climb things instead? Mountains. Passes. Trees. Canyons. Why do I thrive on the freedom and adventure out here?*

"Abnormal" flashed inside my head like a neon sign. I knew now that I could not hike away from it, no matter how hard I tried. I had to change what the sign said.

I don't know anything about what it's like to be an athlete. I don't know what it's like to be normal. I only know what it's like to be me.

I had never thought that I was good enough, fast enough, strong enough, thin enough, pretty enough, smart enough, or any other "enough." Nothing I did had ever met my own unattainable expectations of what "enough" was. *Is that why I threw myself into the hardest physical endeavor I could think of? Was I simply desperate to do something that would make me approve of myself?*

I had noticed some changes in myself, some minute and others enormous. In those moments when I broke my body—or more effectively, my mind—I was discovering how "enough" I really was. It didn't matter to me anymore that someone else might someday hike this trail faster. What mattered was that I was throwing myself against an endurance threshold like it was a brick wall—and I was bruised, not from bouncing off, but from crashing right through it every day.

I reached subalpine Cispus Pass drenched in sweat and warm sunshine. My glutes and hamstrings were burning with the effort of propelling me and my backpack upward toward the sun and sky. The rapid thumping of my heart reverberated in my temples. As I turned to follow the huckleberry-covered ridgeline, the burning in my legs turned to exhilaration as freshly oxygenated blood flooded the muscles. Joy ran through every cell of my body at the sight of the new valley in front of me. Birds in the trees joined their song with that of the water bounding down drainages scattered across the green slopes. Wispy clouds floated overhead and a herd of seventy mountain goats grazed on the slopes above.

I stood motionless—counting every frolicking kid and sturdy mother. They were in their home environment, oblivious to the world of man just a few crow-fly miles away (and several thousand feet below). Finally, I peeled my eyes from them and followed the trail as it circled the head of the valley, crossing the rushing creek. *Did it matter whether or not I was normal if I was happy?*

Hours later—past the narrow, exposed ridgeline called the Knife's Edge—night fell. Unlike previous nights, I walked through the darkness with confidence. I did not jump at every sound even though the forest was alive with unknown animals of all sizes. The Canadian border was less than four hundred miles away and I was on my home turf. Even with my headlamp batteries diminishing in strength, I could still see the trail. Or, at least, I could sense it—a form of familiarity borne of repetition. I had traveled it every night for so long that it was second nature. Instinctively, I walked over rough ground without tripping, moving along the trail like the animal I was—at home in the night.

Eight percent of my body fat had melted over the last twenty-two hundred miles. My physique, rippling with new muscles, was now unfamiliar. I was still a ghost, but now I was also the lioness—lean and strong. The night was my home. I was enough. I roared into the inky blackness, reveling in my power.

CHAPTER 32
NORSE PEAK WILDERNESS, WASHINGTON

DAY 54 / 45 MILES

Myriad chambers of converted sunshine resisted—then gave way to tongue and teeth. A sweet, earthy flavor rolled across my taste buds. I'd tasted this berry somewhere else, in another lifetime when I was young. I remembered my small, violet-stained hands darting between tangled, thorny stalks and pulling berries out by the fistful. Dozens of humid, sweaty days spent fighting through prickly vines in rural Michigan could never be forgotten.

Plunk, plunk, mmmm.

Two for the bucket, one for the mouth. My dad picked nearby—plunk, plunk, plunk. He didn't taste any.

Standing on the PCT, I picked yet another native blackberry and stuffed it into my mouth. There weren't many that were ripe this early, but I could not pass up those that were. Their complex flavor was superior to the broad-leafed blackberry often found intertwined with it—an invader from the Himalaya. I moved a little farther up the trail. A few more blackberries. A handful of ripe huckleberries. *Oil City.* The name came to me as I stopped to pick them.

It was there that dad would take me to pick berries in the heat of summer. My mom would dress me in suffocating layers—sweats that lived up to their name. Dad, though, always wore Dickies—thick, navy-colored pants and long sleeves—with heavy leather boots. He never complained. No doubt he thought the resulting rich berry pie a la mode was worth a sizeable equity in sweat.

Wearing my minimal hiking sundress, I dove into the bushes—my bare arms soon bleeding from scratches. I continued on, scanning more bushes as I hiked. I'd been a forager my entire life, although I'd never thought of it like that until now.

Late summer was for berry picking, but every season brought forth its own harvest. When the first winter snows fell, my father hunted deer for the venison steaks that we ate year round. Through the heart of winter he felled trees to heat our home. Spring meant mushroom hunting.

April in Michigan is a month of cold nights, foggy mornings, and blazing afternoons—morel mushrooms spring from the earth like jacks-in-the-box. I'd follow my dad into the woods with mesh onion bags tucked into my pockets. We'd stand in the semi-shade and stare quietly at the forest floor, waiting. Then, after an eternity of me thinking *there aren't any mushrooms here,* one would appear—my brain having finally deciphered the camouflaged patterns in front of me. I'd stoop to pick its deeply crevassed crown only to see another . . . and another . . . suddenly they were visible everywhere. Later, dad and I would troop home with bulging bags and mom would wash the morels in salt water, coat them in flour, and fry them to perfection.

What I wouldn't give for some fried morels right now.

Just off the trail, a single shriveled thimbleberry clung to a stalk. My eyes—in foraging mode now—spied it from a distance and I pounced as though it would try to run. Even though the berry was long past its prime, the flavor was divine.

Foraging used to mean survival. Now, it was a way of connecting to the natural world as well as an evolutionary past—a delicious reminder of our wild selves. Just like walking thousands of miles, there was something so innately right about wading into the bushes for a perfect, juicy bit of ripeness hanging just out of reach. *Walking long distances, drinking water from the streams, eating the Earth's fruits—this is exactly what humans are meant to do.* I smiled at my berry-stained hands and relished the flavors on my tongue, ready to hike onward through the sliver of Mount Rainier National Park that the PCT traversed.

A few hours later, having passed through the park and crossed over Chinook Pass, I saw, in the gathering dusk, a person I recognized setting up camp under a tree.

"Johnny!" I yelled at the top of my lungs.

He paused and looked my way. "Anish?!"

I ran down the trail, closing the gap between us in a matter of moments. The possibility of hiking company infused me with energy. I hadn't seen Johnny in over a year, not since I'd met him on his last PCT thru-hike when we were both in the tiny trail town of Stehekin.

"Hike with me!"

Johnny looked around at his half set-up camp.

"C'mon! I need the company. I have to hike another thirteen miles tonight. I have to make it to Snoqualmie tomorrow, come hell or high water. C'mon," I urged.

"OK. I just have to pack up."

Standing there, I babbled about the hike so far. I'd known that he was hiking the Pacific Crest Trail again this year. Slowly, I'd gained on him, but he was fast and consistent.

"I didn't know if I'd ever catch you! Are you going to turn around at the border and hike south?"

"Nah, that was something I wanted to do last year. This year I'm just heading home after this."

"I've seen four mountain lions!"

He took his drying clothes off of the tree branches and rolled up his tent. "I'm glad to see they weren't hungry."

Within three minutes he was ready to hike again.

We set off down the trail, taking turns talking rapidly.

"How far did you hike already today? I'm glad you're doing some more miles with me."

"I've done thirty. I'd rather be eating dinner right now, but this is probably the only chance I'm going to get to hike with you. How far did you come today?"

"I think about thirty-three miles, but I feel great! Especially with company. Did you end up going to Italy last winter like you were talking about?"

"No. Just went back to Wisconsin and worked. I was going to do the CDT this year, but there's just something about this trail."

After about ten miles, the excitement waned and we began to slow, both in pace and conversation. Soon, we were reduced to a sleepy shuffle.

"I don't think I can really hike that much farther tonight," I said, stopping and shining my headlamp off to the right.

"Me neither."

"I think there's a flattish spot on the other side of those bushes with room for both our tents."

He followed me as I crashed through the undergrowth.

"Will this work for you?"

"I'm so tired I could sleep on a bed of nails," he replied.

I looked at the time on my phone as I set my alarm for 5 a.m. *Three hours of sleep is enough, I suppose.*

CHAPTER 33

SNOQUALMIE PASS, WASHINGTON

DAY 55 / 53 MILES

Three hours felt like three minutes. My alarm sounded and I scrambled to silence it before Johnny woke up. Still half-asleep, I followed rote memory to pack up and slip past his tent back onto the trail. Dawn broke over an hour later, slightly increasing my cognitive function. I got water from a creek near the small cabin named for Mike Ulrich, built by snowmobilers, and began the prolonged climb up Blowout Mountain. The forest and bushes were damp with dew and low-lying clouds hung in the valleys. It was still the beginning of August, but the perennial moisture of the Pacific Northwest clung to the crest, making the air clammy. Despite the chill, the effort of the climb had me sweating, and I didn't bother to put on my jacket as I circled past the summit. Instead, I hurried back to the shelter of the trees, out of the drifting fog that left goosebumps on my sweaty skin. I knew I'd reached the high point of the day before dropping back into the windless forest.

As I neared tree line I heard a quiet voice: "Hello."

I looked up in surprise to see a man standing there, blocking the trail. He was clad in camo pants, an old T-shirt, and leather boots.

A navy-blue bandanna was tied around his head, and he carried a tiny, thru-hiker-style backpack. At his hip hung a large knife.

"Good morning." I stopped because he hadn't stepped aside off the trail. It was obvious he intended to engage me.

"Are you hiking alone?" He peered around me as if to check for companions.

"No, my boyfriend is a little way back."

"Are you thru-hiking?"

"Yes. What about you?" I tried to steer the uncomfortable conversation away from myself.

"Southbound," he said, not taking the bait. "What is your boyfriend's name?"

"Johnny." I looked him straight in the eye as I lied. I wasn't sure what his intentions were, but his demeanor and line of questioning was terrifying me. But I refused to let him know it, just as I'd refused to back down when face-to-face with a mountain lion.

"When did you start?" I asked.

His pack was that of a thru-hiker, but his clothes and attitude weren't. I had never been afraid to be a woman hiking solo, but now every cautionary tale I'd ever been told raced through my mind. Irrational thoughts, such as wondering if he'd murdered a thru-hiker and taken their pack, sent adrenaline pouring into my bloodstream.

"July 15."

"Oh. Not as much snow for you starting then."

I focused on remaining calm and confident. I kept my tone conversational. *Was he just annoyingly curious? Shouldn't he realize that his questions and appearance could be perceived as threatening to a woman? Stay calm, Anish.*

I knew that I was safer in the woods than on the streets of Seattle, yet his clipped, gruff voice was triggering my gut instinct to get away. His prying questions only added to my fear. *All predators are looking for weakness, Anish. And you are* not *weak.* You're strong. Remember the lion.

"Shouldn't he be right behind you?" The man stepped to one side, searching for the unseen boyfriend.

"He stopped to go to the bathroom on the climb. I'm sure he'll be along soon if you want to chat more with him, but I'm getting cold and need to keep moving."

The man had slightly yielded the trail, and I took advantage of the opportunity to push past him. He called out something, but the blood rushing in my ears prevented me from hearing it. *I need to get away.*

"Have a good hike!" I called back without turning or slowing down.

I focused on walking strong without fleeing—just as I had when the cougar was following me at Myrtle Flat—until I crested the rise and dropped down the other side, out of sight. There I whirled around, expecting to see the man following me. He wasn't there. I leaned against a tree and took several deep breaths. He still didn't appear. I realized that I had just merged with the most runnable section of the Cascade Crest 100 ultramarathon course, a race I had completed two years ago. *If I was able to run the next thirty-eight miles in the midst of a one-hundred-mile race, I can run it now.* I looked up one more time to see if the man had appeared. He hadn't.

I turned northward and I ran.

DAY 56 / 32 MILES

I woke up confused. I was in a bed. The alarm clock read 6 a.m. in bright-red numerals. Suddenly, I remembered the fear and frustration of the day before. The unsettling interaction with a guy on the trail. The fifty-three miles hiked in eighteen hours on only three hours of sleep. How at 10 p.m. I'd been fighting my way through wet vegetation overhanging the trail in the pouring rain. It was 11 p.m. when I'd arrived at the hotel at Snoqualmie Pass and picked up my last resupply box from the woman at the front desk when I checked in.

"I am in Snoqualmie." Somehow my whisper seemed to make it real.

I got up and went about getting myself ready. Two months ago—when I packed that box—I had doubted that I would even make it here to pick it up. Yet, here I was. Ahead of me lay vast tracts of wilderness, where glaciated mountains towered over pristine lakes and deep valleys. The Alpine Lakes and Glacier Peak Wildernesses each held untamed terrain, crossed by the ribbon of dirt that stretched from Mexico to Canada. Beyond that was the North Cascades, where the only access to the outside world was through the boat-in town of Stehekin, the North Cascades Highway, and the dirt road that led to Harts Pass. I was standing on the brink of a remote and wild country—and the end of my journey.

I put my shoes on and got ready to walk out the door. It was almost 7 a.m. I hadn't gotten such a late start since the Saufley's. *"Go get 'em girl!"* Donna's words came to me again. I sank back onto the bed to write one last post. In the wilder regions ahead, I would not have another opportunity to do so. Since the day I'd sat on Mather Pass, talking to a complete stranger, I'd gained thousands of followers on Facebook. It was a mysterious and strange thing to know that so many eyes were watching, and waiting.

I spent hours every day compressing and rewriting in my mind a summary of each forty-five-mile stretch of trail. At night, I further distilled those thoughts into tiny packages of type suitable for the world to see, saving the post on my phone before I fell asleep. Almost daily, I paused long enough at a water break or pass to log in and post my summaries for posterity. I hadn't anticipated that opening up the documentation of my hike to the eyes of the world would leave me feeling invaded. I was in the midst of something incredibly difficult, physically and mentally. And always—out there—people were watching . . . scrutinizing . . . making assumptions and judgments. One time that I read the comments, a single critical statement had fueled my internal foes, despite the hundred encouraging ones.

As much as I wanted to hide from it, though, this was also a precious opportunity to share the essence of what I was learning. If these lessons had helped me, then someone else out there could also benefit from them—someone like me. If I could help them choose to not let fear control their decisions—their lives—then every moment of the hike would be worth it. I picked up my phone and timidly began to type my message to the world.

I imagine people may think I am a natural athlete, the girl who
played sports all through school. The exact opposite is true. I was an

overweight child, a bookworm who sat with her nose in an adventure
book and daydreamed. When I graduated high school, I weighed 200
pounds.

Tears leaked out from the corners of my eyes. The painful parts of my past still had the power to hurt me, but I kept writing.

I daydreamed of adventure, but the thing I daydreamed the most
was that I would someday set a record. Not just any record though, an
athletic record. I wanted so desperately to not be what I was. I hated
my body and myself. I consoled myself by eating bowls full of Oreos
and milk as though they were cereal. But somewhere deep inside I
knew I was capable of doing something more.

When I was 20 I met something that would forever change my
life—a trail. Though my first few hikes were miserable as I forced my
body to work, I was enthralled. Trails took me on the adventures I
craved and to beautiful, wondrous, wild places. I lost my heart and
soul—and eventually 70 pounds—to the trails.

The words flowed more easily as I moved from painful memories to the here and now that made my heart sing—the miles I had walked, the miles I would walk, the woman who found herself in the mountains.

Now, I am a few short days away from fulfilling my oldest day-
dream: setting an athletic record. I cry when I think about all the
things I have overcome to get here, both on this hike and off. It makes
me ever so grateful to that chubby girl who dared to dream big, auda-
cious dreams. I am even more thankful that she grew up to be a woman
courageous enough to make those dreams a reality.

I pressed post and turned my phone off. It was time for the final push to the border.

CHAPTER 34
GLACIER PEAK WILDERNESS, WASHINGTON

DAY 57 / 44 MILES

The trail zigzagged as I descended slopes covered in huckleberry bushes and dripping pines. I was amazed by how the PCT forged a path through the dense forest blanketing Washington State. My back and shoulders burned under the heaviest pack I'd carried since leaving Kennedy Meadows—I was in the middle of the second six-day carry of the hike. The first time I'd carried a pack this heavy, at mile seven hundred, I'd been softer, but with more reserves than now—seventeen hundred miles later. This time, too, the elevation gain in the mountains ahead of me was even more formidable than the Sierra. Thankfully, I didn't have to cope with high altitude.

My body had become a mysterious paradox of total strength and utter weakness. My toe was still swollen, and I hadn't looked at my heel since Willamette Pass. The sores on my back were unbearable—I was constantly picking up sticks and laying them alongside my spine to try and hold the pack weight away from them. The dizziness was gone, but I continued to lose weight. I was glad there were only two hundred miles remaining. I could feel in my marrow that my body was not going to hold out much longer.

The trail had completely exhausted me. Instead of feeling a rush of accomplishment at the top of each pass, I felt only relief. Somehow, though—perhaps it was the adrenaline of being nearly done—I felt almost like the last twenty-three hundred miles had never happened. I didn't feel the same desperate relentlessness to hike fifty miles a day that I did in Oregon, yet I could not help but push past my planned campsites. It didn't seem to matter how chronically fatigued I was or how long it took to cover the miles—my mind simply would not let my body stop until I literally could not walk another step. The result was that I was covering ten or more miles than I had planned every day. I had been a machine before, and now I was something far more primal, the lioness, closing in on the end of my journey. Canada was close and nothing seemed to matter but getting there.

The traffic rolling through Stevens Pass on Highway 2 echoed up to me through the fog. I was cold, even in my rain jacket and gloves. The debilitating heat of the desert felt the many hundreds of miles away that it was. When I finally reached the pavement, the road was empty. To my left lay Seattle, to my right, Leavenworth—I was almost home. The paradox of being so close and yet so far settled over me. I took a deep breath and crossed the highway—a ghost melting into the shadows at the north side of the parking lot.

DAY 58 / 42 MILES

Cumulus clouds coalesced in the sky ahead, billowing upward to seemingly impossible heights. I watched them, thinking of other clouds billowing over cornfields as my dad pointed and explained the differences between cumulus, cirrus, stratus, and their many variations. My father always knew when the rain, tornadoes, snow, or hail would come from the tiniest of signs hidden in the condensed water vapor overhead. I thought of the spelling bee in sixth grade when "cumulus" was the final word I had to spell.

"C, U, M, U, L, U, S," I had said. My voice was shaking despite my confidence—I knew this word as surely as I knew it sprouting in a humid summer sky.

There was a pause that seemed to last an eternity. I watched the inscrutable faces of the four teachers and the principal sitting in the front, presiding over the spelling bee. The eyes of the entire middle school, in the bleachers to my left, were on me. I swore I could hear the eighth-grade girl who'd misspelled her last word breathing where she sat behind me. If I was wrong, she'd get another chance. If I was right, I'd win—and no sixth grader had ever won.

The principal leaned forward to his microphone. "Congratulations. That is correct."

Today, everything my father had ever taught me about the weather told me it was going to storm. Unstable air was circulating around Glacier Peak, hidden in its lair—it was only a matter of time.

I knew the PCT would soon descend to Cady Pass, the lowest point on this stretch, before rising up above tree line, following open ridges for miles to Red Pass. Those ridgeline miles would be fast, but the exposure to the storm could prove dangerous.

As I neared Cady Pass, I noticed movement just down slope, and was surprised to see a man hiking north on the switchback below me. His red braid and sun hat looked so much like Remy that I did a double take. There was only one person it could be.

"Weathercarrot!"

My old friend from the PCT in 2005 turned and his face broke into a huge smile. He waited for me to catch up.

"You know, I never knew your trail name," he said to me. "I didn't even know it was you going after the record until a couple of weeks ago."

I laughed. *The Ghost strikes again.*

"Where are you hiking to?" I asked.

"Doing the northern two hundred miles of the trail before I head down to California to do some work this fall."

At that moment, lightning streaked across the sky. The boom of thunder that followed was almost instantaneous.

"Well, I'm stopping here for the day," Weathercarrot said. "I'm so glad I got to see you. Good luck on the rest of the journey. Stay safe in this storm if you continue on."

"Thanks, I'll try. I have to keep going."

I began to ascend as the heavens hurled lightning and sputtered sleet. When I stopped to look around, there was only the dark underbelly of the cumulonimbus clouds towering above me, with no end in sight. I thought about the storm near The Nipple in California. *Should I continue? Didn't I vow to never put myself in that situation again? Even Weathercarrot stopped and he's hiked many times the number of miles I have.*

In between the cracks of thunder, I heard voices: there were people hiking above me. I headed upward cautiously, rounding the switchback and climbing some more. At the next apex I met a couple who were hastily putting on ponchos. They were laughing, unconcerned about the storm.

"Hi."

"Hello," they answered in unison.

"So, are you heading up?"

"Yeah, to Lake Sally Ann."

"Ah. Not worried about the storm at all?"

The woman looked up, getting a face full of sleet and rain.

"Nah."

"Where are you headed?" the man asked.

"Hiking the PCT. So, Canada."

"So cool! Good luck!"

"Thanks."

I continued past them. Obviously, I was overreacting. Or they were underreacting. Or somewhere in between. Either way, my encounter with them gave me the small boost of courage I needed to keep moving.

The sun had just set by the time I finally crested the rocky saddle of Red Pass. The violence of the storm had diminished to a steady drizzle. Visibility had also diminished to less than fifty feet as fog rolled in. I was glad to have been through this section of trail so many times before—I didn't have to worry about missing the turn down the drainage. I hurried down the open alpine slope and realized that, while my hands were cold, they were not numb. After nearly a decade of Reynaud's attacks, I was surprised and thankful that it had not been an issue on this hike. Nonetheless, I was still freezing cold—movement was the only thing keeping me marginally comfortable. It was a long descent to the White Chuck River and I was hopeful that it would be drier, and hopefully warmer, in the dark bosom of the forest.

CHAPTER 35

NORTH CASCADES NATIONAL PARK, WASHINGTON

DAY 60 / 47 MILES

I woke up, more tired than ever. My body felt weighted to the ground with lead shackles. I rolled over to turn off my alarm and began coughing violently—as though the air was being crushed out of my lungs by the weight of the miles I'd walked. Once it subsided I went through the motions of eating and packing. Finally, I stood there, staring at my pack sitting on the ground—one hundred miles from the Canadian border. Before I'd ever begun this thru-hike, I had fantasized about the moment I would finish. Victoriously sauntering down the trail, I would draw on my ultrarunning skills to push the final one hundred miles to the end, without sleeping. In those daydreams I was strong, defiant, successful—and smiling.

In reality, I was standing with hunched shoulders, loathing my pack. I hated the sores it had rubbed into my body. I hated how it had pulled me backward on every climb of every day. I hated its smell, its filth, its weight. I never wanted to touch it again.

"I hate you!" I screamed and kicked the pack as hard as I could, three times.

Sinking to my knees, I shook with sobs. I was utterly and completely exhausted. A hundred miles or a thousand felt similarly daunting. *All I want to do is sleep.* I knew that it was my choice to be there. Just as it had been my choice every day. I had control of this hike—this destiny. I always had. The record wasn't going to break itself. And there was the vow I'd made to myself at Big Lake Youth Camp when I was certain I could not physically continue. *I am doing what I was meant to do. Nothing will stop me from reaching Canada.*

Sleep deprivation was sending out flares of irrational emotion, but acknowledging the choice, rather than blaming my pack, an inanimate object, allowed me to regain control. *There is something on this path that I still need to do. I have to reach my goal.* I slipped the straps over my shoulders and started walking with the metallic taste of effort lingering in my mouth.

Shortly after noon, I saw a bush overhanging the trail ahead of me twist and shake in the breeze. A few steps later I stopped—there was no breeze. There was only one thing it could be.

"Hey, bear!"

Sure enough, a small black bear leaned out from behind the bushes and looked at me. His large ears twitched and rotated as I clapped my hands. He went back to eating.

"C'mon, bear! I have to get to Canada. You don't understand. Please move."

Normally the sight of a bear would have been enthralling to me, and I would have simply given it space, watching until it left. Today, less than one hundred miles from Canada, I did not want to wait. I jumped up and down, stomping my feet. I clapped and yelled. The bear occasionally looked over at me, but was generally unimpressed by my antics. Tears of frustration rolled down my cheeks. Finally, I started belting out "The Star-Spangled Banner" at the top of my lungs, in a very off-key voice. That did the trick. With what I can only imagine to be the utmost disdain and exasperation a bear can muster, it looked at me for a long minute and then sauntered off uphill. I barely gave it time to disappear into the bushes before I bolted by, still singing.

CHAPTER 36
NORTHERN TERMINUS

60 DAYS, 17 HOURS, 12 MINUTES / 53 MILES

Tears rolled down my cheeks as I strode along Lakeview Ridge, surrounded by the jagged peaks of the North Cascades. Although the light was fading from the sky, I was only seven miles from Canada. I thought of the thousands of people I didn't know who were cheering me on at this very moment. I thought of every mile I had walked in the last sixty days.

Mostly though, I thought of all the years I had rejected myself. I probed the feelings of inadequacy that had plagued me for the past twenty-six hundred miles, and every other day of my life. I'd always questioned why the only thing that made me happy was traveling long distances through the mountains. *Why is it that I can't be content to live a "normal life"? Why do I spiral into depression when I am away from the wilderness for too long? What possible use could my only talent be when it's something as basic as walking? Why am I happiest as a vagabond of the wild?*

The thing that most fulfilled me was selfish, and absolutely useless. Over the years and miles, I'd berated myself. I'd tried to change. I'd tried to settle down. I'd tried to have a career. I'd tried to substitute running for thru-hiking. I'd tried to force myself into any number of conventional molds. I'd prayed—no, I'd demanded—to know why I'd been created like this. *Why did you give me intellect and ability, yet no desire to use either in a meaningful way? Why am I only wired for loving the mountains and moving among them?* In my life—in so many different ways—I had tried. I had tried to become many things. To meet the many external expectations. I had tried to make the world better, to help people. And I had always felt empty.

Now—standing at over six thousand feet on August 7 at 9 p.m.—I remembered the quiet voice of the butterfly, and realized why its answer had stayed with me every day for the last sixty days: "Just walk." Here, on the final day of a crazy journey, doing the thing that came most naturally to me, I knew why I had felt empty before: I needed to be true to myself and my calling.

Being myself—and chasing my dreams—was enough. I never once thought that hiking would make the world better or change a life. Yet, it had. Thousands of people had been inspired. I had learned to accept myself for all that I was and all that I wasn't. My calling came from the mountains and all that I needed to do to answer was put one foot in front of the other.

"This is absolutely the hardest, most beautiful thing I have ever done!" I shouted to distant Mount Baker as the alpenglow faded. *And the most fulfilling.*

I descended from the ridge as night deepened, picking my way down eroded switchbacks. The final miles unfolded as though I were on any other hike. After Castle Pass, the trail became a tangle of brushy overgrowth. I could sense Canada's presence in the void just ahead of me.

"Less than three miles," I whispered over and over to myself. *What will happen to me when I reach the end? What will I do tomorrow when I no longer have to walk?* That unknown was terrifying, but I still felt compelled to get there as quickly as I could.

My legs spun faster and faster until my walk turned into a run. Adrenaline surged through me like a drug. I was so high on it that I felt nothing below my neck—my body having drifted away. I heard my feet pounding the ground and my pack smacking into my back as I ran, but I couldn't feel any of it. I felt nothing but the cool night on my face as I plunged forward. Twice I fell, splayed out facedown like a sea star. My knees crashed into rocks. Each time I arose, shaky and bloody, I felt the sting for a split-second before I took off running again.

At the end of one of those switchbacks, the forest yielded to a yawning swath—the Canadian border. I knew there were two switchbacks left before the monument, and the end of my hike. I ran faster, sprinting. I surged into the swath, expecting cheers and hugs from friends. Instead, my unearthly shriek echoed in the empty darkness. Sixty days of adrenaline, pain, fear, courage, drive, joy, relief, and sadness were ripped from my lungs and released into the night.

Then came a volley of violent sobs that shook my whole body. I stood with my hands braced against the pillars, the brown twins of the white columns at the Mexican Border, for thirty seconds. I let the waves crash over me and tried simply to breathe. When I could finally inhale and exhale without convulsing, I hefted the top off of the smaller, metal monument. I fished out the ziplock that held a journal and pen and sank to the ground to count the calendar days on my phone. Inside the journal, I scrawled words I had been writing in my head since the Mexican border—the story of a journey taken to find one's self on a mountainside. Once I set them free, on a damp piece of notebook paper, I, too, was free of their weight.

I closed the book and left behind the message I'd carried through long days and short nights. It would wait for those that came after me to read—a phantom benediction. Then I snapped a couple of pictures, put everything back as it was, and turned and walked into Canada—leaving the monument seemingly untouched. Leaving the trail exactly as a ghost would, as though I had never been there.

EPILOGUE

I slept for fifteen hours straight when I finally reached my own bed, dreaming for the first time since I'd begun my hike. I dreamed of hiking, of walking . . . endless walking through the dark. My path illuminated by the dim beam of a dying headlamp. The ground littered with snakes—beautifully banded in black and orange. I hopped over and maneuvered around them, not knowing if they were venomous. I was terrified. Yet I kept going. I woke up knowing that courage would always triumph over fear, even in my darkest dreams.

Initially I was so very glad to no longer have to stumble into the night. To not have to push forward, trying to reach an arbitrary destination before I slept. Eventually, I came to miss those nights, even though they were the hardest. They were when I came to terms with my fears and wrestled with my determination—I learned to fight the desire to give up. Those nights were cold and slow, and I both dreaded and relished them. They had scarred me, but the scars from those nights would remind me to be strong always—until my death.

Days passed differently off-trail. They had no rhythm and more choices. As the August sunshine faded to autumnal gold I found myself fading too. I grieved the loss of the trail. I no longer woke up exactly where I was supposed to be with no decisions to make except to hike on. I missed the repetitive freedom of the trail. I yearned for the power and the despair—the growth and the connection to my primitive self.

That is how, night after night, I found myself sitting next to half-eaten bags of chocolate chips with an empty aching in my soul. My head swirled with negative emotions—the same ones I'd battled with since I was young. When I looked into the mirror—still a size 0 from the starvation of the trail—I saw a stranger that I didn't know.

I knew I was not physically well. I needed to rebuild my body. My doctor had encouraged another blood test and I'd refused. I had just run my already anemic body into the ground. Numbers would only show just how much. I shouldn't have attempted a record when my ferritin levels were barely scraping 20. I hated to think what they were now.

I spent hours on my phone, scrolling through my photos and journals from the Pacific Crest Trail. Along with the dreadlocks that had formed over the many miles, it was the only connection I had to the trail. The only connection I had to a force that had changed my life. I felt a homesickness I could never explain. I was completely disconnected from what I'd done and how I had felt. For two months I had lived for a singular goal worth risking my life, relationships, resources, and health for. Now that I had been off of the trail for twice that long, I was lost and directionless—hollow and void.

Slowly, the demons I thought I had silenced returned to fill that void.

"You've run. You've climbed. You've placed well. You hold a record, but it means nothing."

Over and over I was invited to talk about my accomplishment. I knew that I had inspired others. I had thousands of followers online and in person. My friends looked at me differently, but I was disconnected from all of them. It was as though a Ghost had walked the trail, but I had not. Now I was trying to live her life while she was still out there, resting beneath the softly falling snow.

I tried, yet I couldn't recall the discomfort. I couldn't remember the way bone-deep fatigue felt. I could no longer singularly focus my mind on a goal. Now, it ran rampant, following every passing thought. Worst of all, I was no longer fearless. I worried that I would be discovered. That someday everyone would realize that I was not the elite athlete they believed I was. I felt like I had finally proven that I was capable of something . . . and still I couldn't believe in myself.

"You were the benefactor of luck alone. You don't have what it takes to be the best at anything. You're too fat. Too slow. Too ugly. You're sick and weak. There is no way that you did what you did by your own ability. You know you don't deserve admiration. It was an accident. You could never do it again." My internal demons taunted me every day, morning and night.

I was another person when I was on that trail—one completely obsessed and driven, compelled by a love of wilderness and finding her limits. Now, I felt soft and empty, homesick and restless. I remembered the almost insurmountable struggle of those sixty days—but I would do anything to be there again.

I picked up the remnants of the bag of chocolate chips and threw them into the trash. Awash in emotions I couldn't even articulate, all I knew for certain was that I needed to go. I needed to walk away from everything and keep walking. I needed to go into wilderness and never return. I needed the life of a nomad, the discipline of determination—and I needed it to last more than just two months. I craved the intensity, even though I knew it might eventually destroy me. It was the only thing that could fill the void left by the Pacific Crest Trail.

I wanted to remember. I wanted to forget. I closed the album of PCT photos on my phone. Then I threw it across the room. I screamed. Then I sank down onto the floor with my knees to my chest, hands wrapped around my head as I wept. My fingers coiled into the dreads that still crowned my skull. They held the memories of the blood, the sweat, and the tears.

I reached for the scissors sitting on a nearby table. I held them against a handful of locks like a knife to a throat. I set them back down. I thought about deleting my photos and erasing the journal that I was trying to forge into a book. I had once thought that if I failed to set that record I would throw my identity away and start over. Unexpectedly, success also made me want to forget everything—forget that I had set a record at all—walk away, and start over.

I knew I couldn't erase the memories. Even if I did, the void would swallow me completely. My despair was interlaced with wild grandeur and strength—rebirth carved along a mountain path. My life was now woven from the experience, a cloth created from beauty as well as struggle.

"I am who I am and that person is OK. I do what I do because of who I am and what I am meant to be. The wild brings me insurmountable blessing and joy. It makes sense that when I leave it to eke out my survival in society, I spiral into despair."

I whispered the first cogent summation of my experience. One word at a time, I wrote it down so I could hold it close when I felt like the world was ending. I was finding that it took more strength to maintain my sanity in the face of post-hike depression than it ever had to set a speed record.

I'd been through the rite of passage that was post-thru-hike depression three times before, but never so severe. I knew that something had to give way—it always did. I knew that someday, when the tsunamis inside of me had receded, I would remember how to be Anish both on-trail and off.

ACKNOWLEDGMENTS

A great deal of time and foot dragging preceded the writing of this book. I owe it to my many friends, followers, and family for pushing me to put this story to paper. There were many moments after the summer of 2013 when I wished to forget everything that had happened. I never set out to prove anything to the world, much less become trail famous. It is because of the encouragement of so many that I had the courage to relive, and write down, every dark and triumphant moment of those two months.

I would like to offer a special thank you to Barney "Scout" Mann. You are not only a trail angel of the highest order, but you were instrumental in the creation of this text—you listened with compassion to my sobbing phone calls when I wanted to forget. It's because of you that I chose to journal instead, eventually leading me to create a book for the world to read.

Much gratitude to my mother, Beverly. When I would bring you scribbled stories written in block letters with crayon, you took me seriously. Throughout high school and college you were my editor and proofreader. Without you I would have long ago given up my dream of being a published author.

Thank you to my partner, Adam, for putting up with my stress, long hours in front of the screen, and frequent requests to listen to revisions. I love you.

A huge thank you to my friends who read various iterations and revisions over the years and offered constructive criticism. You helped me see the things I'd missed and confirmed the story I was trying to tell.

I owe a lot to the trail community. Without you, I may have never found my place in this world. To the Pacific Crest Trail Association, trail crews, and trail angels that create and maintain these footpaths that we walk and the community along them, thank you from the bottom of my heart.

Most importantly, the greatest thanks go to Kirsten Colton, Kate Rogers, and Mountaineers Books. I came to you with only a vague outline for the narrative I needed to tell and an impossible schedule, yet you coaxed the best possible story out of my heart. Despite my nomadic lifestyle you worked with me to create something I never could have on my own. Your contributions to this work are invaluable.

ABOUT THE AUTHOR

Heather Anderson, known as Anish on trail, is the second woman to complete the "Double Triple Crown of Backpacking," hiking the Appalachian, Pacific Crest, and Continental Divide National Scenic Trails twice. She holds overall self-supported Fastest Known Times (FKTs) on the Pacific Crest Trail (2013)—hiking it in 60 days, 17 hours, 12 minutes, breaking the previous men's record by four days and becoming the first woman to hold the overall record—and the Arizona Trail (2016), which she completed in 19 days, 17 hours, 9 minutes. She also holds the women's self-supported FKT on the Appalachian Trail (2015) with a time of 54 days, 7 hours, 48 minutes. She is also the first woman to complete the Triple Crown in a calendar year.

Heather has hiked more than thirty thousand miles since 2003, including thirteen thru-hikes. An ultramarathon runner, she has completed six 100-mile races since August 2011 as well as dozens of 50-kilometer and 50-mile events. She has attempted the infamous Barkley Marathons four times, starting a third loop once. Heather is also an avid mountaineer working on several ascent lists in the US and abroad.

Follow her adventures at anishhikes.wordpress.com and @anishhikes.